AT HOME
IN THE WOODS

D1474321

AT HOME
IN THE WOODS

Living the Life of Thoreau Today

BRADFORD ANGIER AND VENA ANGIER

Camden, Maine

Published by Down East Books
A wholly owned subsidiary of The Rowman & Littlefield Publishing Group, Inc.
4501 Forbes Boulevard, Suite 200, Lanham, Maryland 20706
www.rowman.com

Unit A, Whitacre Mews, 26-34 Stannary Street, London SE11 4AB

Distributed by NATIONAL BOOK NETWORK

British Library Cataloguing in Publication Information Available

Library of Congress Cataloging-in-Publication Data

ISBN: 978-1-60893-442-3 (pbk.: alk. paper)
ISBN: 978-1-60893-443-0 (electronic)

♾️™ The paper used in this publication meets the minimum requirements of
American National Standard for Information Sciences—Permanence of Paper for
Printed Library Materials, ANSI/NISO Z39.48-1992.

Printed in the United States of America

DEDICATION

For the Gethings, Dudley Shaw, Ambroses, Bakers, Barkleys, Bazeleys, Beatties, Blairs, Boes, Borings, Boyntons, Campbells, Bill Carter, Fred Chapman, Chapples, Bob Clarke, Curries, Cuthills, Ellises, Fells, Garbitts, Gaylors, Teddy Green, Hamiltons, Holdens, Johnsons, Bill Keily, Gus Krossa, Krugers, Kyllos, Macdonalds, MacDougalls, McFarlands, Marshall Miller, Murphies, Hugh Murray, Ohlands, Pecks, Pickells, Pollons, Robisons, Rosses, Rutledges, Wyndham Smith, Stotts, Stan Wallace, Wegens, Bob Yeomans, and our other friends and neighbors of Hudson Hope.

CONTENTS

ILLUSTRATIONS

CHAPTER ONE

ADVENTURING ON LIFE

We went to the wilderness because 100 years ago a man wrote a book. We'd been putting off going for a long time. It had seemed the only sensible thing to do. Now the century-old sentences mocked us. Why, they taunted, should we waste the best years of our lives earning money in order to enjoy a questionable freedom during the least valuable part?

"Times have changed," I tried to laugh that decisive afternoon, but here was another paragraph that seemed even more true in this complex age than it could have been a century before.

The mass of men lead lives of quiet desperation, the volume incanted. They make themselves sick that they may lay up something against a sick day. Their incessant anxiety and strain is a well-nigh incurable form of disease. It is a fool's life. Yet it appears they honestly believe no choice is left.

"But no way of thinking or doing, however ancient, can be trusted without proof." My husband read with slow significance. "What people say you can not do, you try and find you can."

Henry David Thoreau had gone to the woods in 1845 because he wanted to reduce existence to its essentials and learn what life really had to offer. He dwelled alone for two

11

years and two months, a mile from any neighbor, on the rustic shore of Walden Pond in Concord, Massachusetts. This robust experiment in serene living had convinced him of one thing. To maintain oneself on this earth is not a hardship but a pastime, he found, if one will live simply and wisely.

"It is some advantage to lead a primitive life, though in the midst of civilization, if only to learn what are the necessaries," Thoreau determined. "Most of the luxuries and many of the so-called comforts are not only dispensable, but positive hindrances. Our life is frittered away with detail."

"But that was a hundred years ago," I felt bound to object. "Have you ever inched past Walden Pond on a warm Sunday? The pioneers there now wear bathing suits, and a lot of them chase girls around parked automobiles. When they get hungry, they buy hot dogs and potato chips."

"There's still wilderness somewhere," Brad smiled, "and why shouldn't they chase them? Isn't that why the girls run?"

The Alaska Highway was in the news—over 1500 magic and miraculous miles, the sole overland route to a fabulous frontier as large as all Europe west of pre-war Russia. The normal population of these million-and-a-third square miles of oil, gold, and uranium would hardly fill the Rose Bowl for a New Year's football game.

"How about the Alaska Highway?" Brad insisted. "There's still room somewhere for two more."

"We haven't managed to get much money ahead yet," I answered automatically. "We couldn't get away now, anyway. Our jobs. . . . In a few years, maybe. . . ."

"That's what we keep telling ourselves, Vena," I heard him say dully.

Nervous Back Bay traffic clattered and shrieked outside, lifting dust and fumes into Boston's already hazy atmosphere. When Brad extended one long arm and slammed a window, papers rattled near his typewriter where he hadn't finished that week's news for the theatrical business magazine of which he was New England editor. One yellow sheet swooped behind my rawhide makeup case, already packed so that I could seize it the moment the booker's car arrived to take me to rehearsal at the theatre where I was producing musical shows.

Between us lay an aged edition of *Walden*, Thoreau's classic of which nearly everyone has heard but which few alive have read. Its rugged sentences—whose significance grows with the years, as what is called our advancing civilization becomes increasingly frenzied—seemed to push aside the sooty noisiness of railroad yards and the clamor of automobiles paced by Commonwealth Avenue's red and yellow and green lights.

The cost of a thing is the amount of life which is required to be exchanged for it, immediately or in the long run, Thoreau reasoned. When one has obtained those essentials necessary to well being—food, shelter, warmth, and clothing—there is an alternative to struggling for the luxuries. That's to adventure on life itself, one's vacation from humbler toil having commenced.

The words might have been written tomorrow instead of ten decades ago. Aren't most men still needlessly poor all their lives because they think they must inhabit a home like their neighbors? Consider, Thoreau encouraged, how slight a shelter is necessary. Before it became unfashionable, a comfortable home was made on this continent almost entirely of such materials as nature furnished ready to hand.

The noise of the aging city was all around us. Yet a woodland stillness seemed gentle in the room, as if some part of those bygone days had not entirely gone. A page rustled. For an instant it was as if the apartment echoed with the whir of a saw and the ring of an ax freeing aromatic bark from moist white trunks. Then I heard my voice, louder than usual and almost harsh.

"We couldn't build a cabin for $28 today," the words objected.

"A lot of trappers and prospectors still put them up for less," Brad said very carefully, "although a dollar now is worth one-fourth of what it was in Thoreau's time. It depends where we decide to live, Vena."

"How," the voice pressed and became tenser, "how about food? Neither of us could possibly exist on the twenty-seven cents a week Thoreau apologized for spending."

"We've got to go where meat is free for the hunting, fish for the catching, fuel for the cutting, land for the settling, and a home for the fun of building." His blue eyes seemed to be looking a long way off. "People talk about the *good old days* as if they're something in the past. Up off the Alaska Highway, right here on this continent, there's thousands of square miles that haven't even been walked upon yet."

The inevitableness of what was going to happen lay naked before me then. I don't know why what I saw left me so completely calm.

"You really want to go this time, don't you, Brad?" I said. It interested me to experiment with the inflection of every syllable, because it was as if I were two people and one was amused with the other.

"Maybe we've already put it off too long. It's become a habit." His tall body seemed gaunt with the natural yearning of that part of our most primitive ancestor which survives within us. "Let's make a home with our own hands, Vena. We've enough saved to carry us through a few months. Maybe it's not much, but it's more than Thoreau had. By the time that nestegg's spent, perhaps we can earn enough by writing."

"Writing about what?" I thought, and I must have said it aloud.

"A lot of other folks are dreaming about an escape to some paradise, too," he considered. "Yes, just dreaming and letting it go at that. It might make a difference to them if what Thoreau proved a century ago about returning to nature would still work today. That's it, Vena. Let's put Thoreau to the test."

"We could always pick up here where we leave off, I suppose," I said automatically, although I wondered as detachedly just how easy that would be.

The raucousness of an automobile horn intruded upon the almost breathless impression of stillness. Other familiar noises beat with growing insistence against the suspended illusion of my consciousness, and I realized I was already grasping the makeup case while pressing remorselessly to my feet.

"How soon, Brad?"

"No use putting it off," he seemed to hesitate, still untouched by the interruption. "A month?"

"I'll tell the office not to take any more bookings. We'll have to shop, pack, plan, and I don't know anything about the woods. . . ."

"We'll learn fast enough," he chuckled.

"All right, you can laugh." I caught a ragged breath. "But at least, we'll be going some place where you'll need me as terribly as I need you."

"Darling," Brad was saying. "Why, darling, there's no reason to be upset."

"A lot of husbands and wives don't really need each other in the city." The words, crowding one another, seemed unfamiliar, for I hadn't realized I had been thinking that way. "Don't we see it all around us? There's always restaurants, hotels, and a woman who'll come in to clean. If it gets too lonesome, there's always someone else in a city."

"Why, darling," Brad said, and it didn't sound like him, either. "It isn't as if we haven't been talking about this for a long time. There's no reason to be upset."

The horn blared insistently outside. The book kept the

hopeless and yet always hopeful bustle away from him a few moments more. He was holding me close, and he still clutched the antiquated volumn in one hand.

"See," my husband indicated. His assurance maintained a fiber of illusion still intact. As he read, Thoreau's calm sincerity appeared to cheer the apartment. " 'I learned this, at least, by my experiment. If one advances confidently in the direction of his dreams, and endeavors to lead the life which he has imagined, he will meet with a success unexpected in common hours.' "

My voice picked up the shining old strands, entwining them more surely in today's entangled tapestry with every word.

" 'If you have built castles in the air, your work need not be lost. That is where they should be. Now put the foundations under them.' " As I echoed Thoreau's serene philosophy, my vision somehow became bright with the relief of tears. "Oh, darling, darling. We will make our dreams come true!"

CHAPTER TWO

THE BRIDE GOES NORTH

The train, after a series of jerks that lengthened into one great rumbling motion, clackity-clack-clack-clacked out of the old echoes that seem always to linger in the North Station. Hard pellets of snow stung frosting windows. Softer flakes eddied after the cars on a sharp damp wind, as sweet with not unpleasant distillery odors as any that had sent privateers scudding out of Boston Harbor in the adventuresome days before the city started losing its shipping.

The locomotive punctuated its metallic plunge through February darkness with a series of shrieks. Red lights, somewhere in the deepening cold outside, reflected on the door of our bedroom. The reservations across the continent had been a going-away present; a sybaritic sendoff, I thought now, to a pioneer existence.

The racket of the train surged momentarily louder. A figure, not at once familiar, shouldered through a yellow wedge of brightness from the squeaking corridor. The accompanying draft sent my rust jersey slithering against already chilled legs. Brad, clicking the door behind him, seemed almost as surprised as I at the desperateness with which I sought his warmth. It was as if, for an uncertain instant, he was my only sanctuary in a whirling frigid universe.

17

The realization stared at me that I was speeding farther and farther from the accustomed although often tiresome bounds that, probably because of that very shortcoming, I had come to associate with security. Isolation seemed to lie ahead, somewhere beyond the edge of my world. Suddenly, I wasn't adventuresome any more. No longer was this a comfortable armchair reverie. A monster of my own creation had come dominatingly alive.

"Oh, Brad," a small and desperate tone pleaded in the tumultuous darkness.

The nearly hysterical note in my voice made me feel such a fool. It was that very shame which steadied me. Pioneering is something women have to work up to gradually, I began to scold myself. Even the sturdiest of our covered wagon ancestresses probably faltered while still within sight of the old homes they maybe loathed but to which they clung instinctively, because a part of their earlier years that could never be retrieved would always remain shackled there.

"It's going to be all right, Brad," I said more softly.

A local thundered by in the opposite direction. It shattered the already monotonous rumble so abruptly that I could not conceal a tremor which, the next instant, I was hoping he would lay to affection. Amber coach windows bobbed past. A stanch arm braced my shoulders reassuringly. Mingled with the clatter of someone moving by in the aisle outside came the sound of my husband drawing in a deep breath, and then I found myself pressing swimming eyes unashamedly against his rough clean tweeds.

"Sure," my husband said at last, and his very voice was part of the calmness I sought. "Sure, Vena. It's going to be a whole lot better than anything you and I have ever imagined."

Montreal was feathery with falling snow, as we climbed the long hill from Bonaventure Station the next morning.

The last high heels I expected to wear for months slipped on ice caked inches thick on the sidewalks. I caught at Brad's arm the instant he scrambled for mine, and then there it was—laughter, the release of carefree light-hearted laughter, for the first time in days.

This was a wintry new world I realized, as I really looked about me for the first time. This was beyond turning back. The old ordinary days with their chaining habit-patterns were in the past. The tedious hours of outfitting for this new life all lay behind. So did the ritual of parties. So did the pang of getting rid of everything but the most essential. So did the farewells that seemed the more poignant because most of them had to reach so voraciously for sincerity. The old ways were beneath an already dimming horizon. Promising fresh paths were emerging, bright and irresistible.

Our six bulging duffle bags, the trunks of the farther places, had just been passed without incident by one of the thoughtful customs officials who make the crossing of Canada's borders always the more gracious. I had been dreading the task of ever cramming everything back into them after the inspection, but there had been little need to worry.

"What is in them, please?" the blue-garbed officer had asked courteously, walking around the load that occupied a baggage truck of its own.

My mind spun. I glanced helplessly at Brad. He was occupied in unstrapping his eiderdown sleeping robe in the softness of which was rolled the big-game rifle with its telescopic sight, the lighter .250-3000 carbine, and the little .22 repeater whose serial numbers all had to be checked. I tried to think of how to describe the contents of the duffle bags in something less than an hour.

There was the electrifying odor of locomotive smoke, and the muffled call of "All aboard" reminded me that the

larger portion of our journey loomed excitingly in the near
future if I could ever get past this barrier. The man from the
customs office was copying information from a tag.

My thoughts struggled to form a logical pattern of the
things we'd painstakingly selected, and at the same time to
subtract mentally the far larger heap we'd adamantly declared surplus and left behind.

Women are unsuited, both in nature and experience I
realized anew, when it comes to outfitting for the wilderness.
Brad had enthused to me one morning, across a heap of
magazines and catalogs, that every trip back of beyond is
divided into three delightful segments; the joy of getting
ready, the adventure itself, and finally the pleasure of
reminiscing. I'd never experienced the latter two phrases,
so I couldn't form any logical opinion about them. But the
first, I soon became aware, could be a nightmare.

It had been bad enough after the first few indecisive
shopping trips to paw through scratchy woolen breeches,
heavy itchy sox, and irritating durable shirts when I'd much
rather have been choosing sheer, gay frivolities. I had finally
put my foot down as far as clothing was concerned.

"Granted," I had said, "that woolens are practical during
cold weather and warm, wet days and dry. But I'm not in
training to become a female Paul Bunyan. Granted, too,
that riding gear if chic is too tight for walking. There's my
morale to think of. Woolens can still be pretty, soft, and
feminine. We'll just go around to that ski shop."

All this flashed before my eyes now, as the customs
official waited. I also remembered a confusion of too many
details that had to do with our amassing such necessities as
maps, cheap watches for everyday use, sun glasses, ammunition, candles, rubber-bottomed leather boots, a barometer
for forecasting the weather, Brad's worn binoculars, a pair
apiece of unbreakable waterproof match cases, carefully
selected books, fishing tackle, small tools, a folding shovel,

first aid kit, toilet articles, canteens, a leather-sheathed 2½ pound ax, a 100-foot coil of ⅜ inch manila rope, sewing materials, eiderdowns, air mattresses, compact rubber pump to inflate the latter, wire, knives, pocket carborundums, compasses, tent, light waterproof tarpaulin, two mosquito bars, collapsible frying pans, two canvas buckets, flashlights, a general repair kit of small odds and ends such as safety pins and rubber cement, and writing materials.

It was with especial pride that I recalled my part in the acquisition of a beautiful little aluminum-steel nested cooking outfit that—inside its round waterproofed container, eight inches across and five inches deep—amazingly held no less than five plates, three cups, three soup bowls, shallow pan and capacious pot with covers for both, frying pan, salt and pepper shakers, can opener, silverware for three, and the neatest teakettle I'd ever seen. The cups were made of stainless steel which, Brad had already proved to me, were as cool to the lips as fine porcelain.

This pleasure of ownership had helped to offset the despair I'd felt when it had been jointly decided to leave other articles behind because we couldn't spare the weight nor space. I'd sneaked in several afterwards, more forlornly than rebelliously.

The National Revenue representative was regarding me with politely inquiring eyebrows.

"Oh, goodness," I said helplessly, "there's our clothing, and sleeping bags, and cooking things, and. . . . and . . ."

"Personal belongings," he suggested, running a sensitive Gallic hand along one bag, "and household effects?"

"That's it exactly," I agreed with relief.

He made note of such specific items among our hand luggage as the small 1.4 volt battery radio, portable typewriter, and our Leica camera with its f2 Summitar lens and accessories that included a self timer. Then without requiring us even to open those distended duffle bags he handed us an entry permit which, he smiled hospitably, we could have periodically renewed without charge merely by writing customs.

The morning was still early when these few formalities were completed. He verified our compartment reservations across the continent to make sure everything was in order. Even though they had been a gift, our funds were already so small that as we awaited our turn at the window I had the impulse to ask if we couldn't ride in the coaches instead. Brad had the same sobering thought, he admitted later. Neither of us had wanted to be the one to suggest it. Besides, although I knew we would cheerfully rough it whenever the occasion demanded, we both liked whatever the particular best might be at any given time. This was a sort of honeymoon, too. We'd been too busy to take a real one the nearly two years before.

The Continental Limited wouldn't leave until that evening. We had all day to explore Montreal. Happily, I linked arms with my husband.

"Free, free, free," my elevator spikes seemed to tap. We had made the break. We were adventuring on life. "We were free, free, free, and on our way!"

CHAPTER THREE

END OF THE STEEL

Thousands of stars glowed in an Alberta sky more blue than black when three mornings later the porter handed us down from the Continental Limited at the 100th Street Station in Edmonton. There were the usual knots of people, and an aged employee was dragging a hand truck noisily across some tracks. I felt excitedly alive.

What wind there was had a clean, unfettered quality that spoke of unmapped mountains, unexplored forests, and great rivers winding northward with an inevitableness that became even more serene the nearer they roiled toward the luring Pole. I filled my lungs with brisk air. After four nights in sleepers, it seemed as if I still swayed with the motion of the train.

"Isn't Edmonton flat?" I noted, as we walked the few blocks to the lighted business district. "And dark? That's because we're so far north, isn't it? Isn't this the northernmost city on the continent? And we're still traveling toward the Arctic?"

"We catch the last of our trains late this afternoon," Brad nodded. "It'll take another night and day to ride to the end of the line. Say, are you as hungry as I am?"

The end of the steel! The jumping-off place! Dawson

Creek, British Columbia, was these. I could feel eyes following us when we swung off the Northern Alberta Railways' *Muskeg Limited* after a jolting night and day. They were curious eyes but friendly. Fortunes in mineral and fur flowed through this railhead each year. Probably these people were wondering what beckoned us to the vast wild lands beyond. There seemed to be a comradeship in the unspoken curiosity.

Selecting a wilderness niche is, I'd found, a highly individual matter. Much of it depends upon what one wants most and upon the compromises, accordingly, one is willing to make. We had set for our goal a high and open forested country. Initial distance did not matter, although it appeared only sensible that a store and post office should be reasonably accessible. Cold was no obstacle, either, but we did desire a semi arid climate where there would not be a lot of snow and rain. There didn't seem to be any reason for going someplace where flies and mosquitoes would be too pestiferous, either. We had to limit our choice, finally, to primitive wilderness where a home would be free for the making and where there'd be an abundance of fish and game.

When one has settled upon as many non-conflicting requirements as possible, we found that scanning maps and talking to acquaintances "who've been there" may help to turn the trick. Voluminous information, too, can be obtained by writing the tourist bureaus that are located in state and provincial capitals. One may state his problem frankly as we did to the Department of Interior in Washington, D. C., and to the Government Travel Bureau in Ottawa, Ontario. Letters to leading outdoor magazines brought us surprisingly interested suggestions. Moreover, we found the eager tourist representatives of the several railroads to which we wrote well supplied with details. Maybe here's the place for us to thank, as we do sincerely, Arthur W. Holman, D. Leo Dolan, William H. Currie, Ernest Evans, F. R.

Butler, Dave Griffiths, Dr. F. H. McLearn, and the others who gave us kind and valuable assistance.

Adjectives will be necessarily discounted in most cases. Conclusions will be drawn from temperature charts, forestry reports, contour maps, rainfall tables, frost graphs, wild-life surveys, botanical lists, and other such concrete factors. The procedure, I hoped, would prove sound in our case. We had done all these things with painstaking exactness before agreeing, "Hudson Hope must be the place for us."

The outfitting point for a north woods location so chosen will probably have commercial lodgings of sorts. If it is to remote for that, there's bound to be a family who'll welcome travellers for a few days just for the opportunity to talk with someone from Outside. I'll never forget our own arrival. . . .

The graveled 36-foot-wide Alaska Highway was a pleasant surprise when we left the next afternoon, although the descent to the span across the Peace River took my breath. After passing the outskirts of Fort St. John, the truck jounced westward up a dirt road. The vehicle was heavy with Indian freight, later to be conveyed by horse from Hudson Hope to free trader and Indian Department rep-resentative Teddy Green on the Graham River. Brad had arranged the ride for us with a minute's conversation after hours of scouting through the Dawson Creek garages in search of transportation.

The truck kept skidding around unprotected curves as if they didn't matter. It might have been like swooping along a roller coaster track, except that amusement park rides have safety straps and at least an excuse for a railing.

"Didn't used to be nothing but a horse trail in here until a little while ago," the driver commented with some pride, as we passed a group of deserted cabins. "The Geth-ings, who have some coal mines up at the Hope, had a lot to do with putting in the road. Say, I sure hope the Hump ain't going to be too slippery for this here corn-binder."

The vehicle did have difficulty getting over the young mountain that our chauffeur conservatively termed the Hump. Whenever the laboring wheels skidded to the left of what passed for a road, there was the Peace River hundreds of feet almost straight down. The dark youthful driver —and as Brad enthused, that sourdough could really wheel—wanted to know, surprisingly, wasn't the icy ribbon beautiful in the frosty moonlight with the Northern Lights acting up that way? We'd already come about 140 miles. There was Hudson Hope ahead, although the "bucket of bolts" would have to wheeze up Lynx Creek hill before we could see it, and did I hear those coyotes?

The log cabins of Hudson Hope, snug beneath the Aurora Borealis, clustered restfully about one of the fur trading posts of the nearly three-century-old Hudson's Bay Company. A trail sparkled beside its trim white buildings to where a great spring gushed out of the slope dropping toward the Peace River.

A small log hotel, opening wide a hospitable door at the sound of our tires in crusted snow, seemed the most beautiful I had ever seen. A snapping fire, hot food that Mr. and Mrs. Robert Ferguson hastened to prepare, and incredibly peaceful surroundings combined soporiferously with the relaxing knowledge that we'd neared our journey's end. I actually dozed over my coffee. Brad put a supporting arm about me as we trudged up the stairs.

"After nearly a week of traveling," he sympathized, "no wonder you're tired. Tomorrow morning you just sleep yourself out."

The iron shoes of two horses, hauling a creaking sleigh, awoke me out of what seemed like drugged slumber the next morning. They seemed to be clicking musically down the broad white road outside our bedroom window. I half-lifted myself on one elbow. A round man, with merry round eyes and unruly black hair that a stocking cap seemed only to toss more askew, was perched on a plank that slanted across the two side boards. A small yellow dog circled the team officiously.

"Hey, Ted," a man in a tweed suit and a glossy fur hat called from the doorway of what was evidently a store.

The round man reined his horses to a prancing standstill and disappeared cheerfully after the second individual whom he identified as, "Dave."

Hudson's Bay Company, the sign above the door announced in Old English letters. Beneath this in smaller printing was the legend, "Incorpopated 2nd May 1670."

With a disregard of trifles befitting a concern that had been a century old before the United States was more than an absent-minded dent in one of Paul Revere's teapots, no one had bothered to add the corrective stroke to the erroneous "P."

There across from the hotel, neatly tied together by a chaste picket fence, clustered the traditionally red-roofed white buildings of one of the some 200 posts still operated in the North by the world's oldest trading corporation. The sight crowded my mind with visions of baled furs, of huge freight canoes, and of brightly sashed French Canadian voyageurs singing beneath their loads.

Brad shouldn't be sleeping through all this, I thought. As I was turning to arouse him, the door across the street reopened. Brad walked out into the snow accompanied by the man in the fur hat and the round driver of the sleigh. He pointed questioningly upriver. Both strangers nodded. Before I could call, my husband strode rapidly out of sight in that direction.

CHAPTER FOUR

FAMILY IN THE FOREST

"I've found it!" my husband exclaimed ten hours later, and his voice had a bite like that of the evening air that coursed after him into the rustic lobby. Coils of vapor, condensed by the frigidity, swirled momentarily in the heat of the hotel stoves. Brad appeared to consider them before amending, "That is, I think we have found it."

The HB.C. manager had told him that morning about a place a prospector had built upriver on government land, then deserted upon moving to always more promising diggings. It was free for the occupying, David M. Cuthill had said, like so many other forsakened shelters in the immense and incredible subarctic. Best of all, Brad went on almost hastily, here was perhaps the location where we'd want to raise our own log walls.

"Thoreau had a pretty sound viewpoint about that," Brad added more calmly. "Do you recall how Thoreau noted that at a certain season of our life we're accustomed to consider every spot as the possible site of a house? He recommended Cato's yardstick, remember? 'The oftener you go there, the more it will please you if it is good.' "

"So when do we go there for our first look?" I managed to interrupt.

It might be a pretty long hike for someone who was already fagged the way I must be, Brad explained carefully. The place was a few miles upriver, just below Box Canyon. It might even be as far as six miles actually, although I'd never think of it as that far when I started walking along the interesting riverside trail.

It so happened, as a matter of fact, that Ted Boynton was going to drive his sleigh that way tomorrow. Ted had backed up everything Dave said about the place, and maybe we could ride along with him if we wanted. It might just happen that the sleigh would be empty. If so, why didn't we throw in our duffle bags in case we wanted to stay?

As a matter of fact, he'd thought of picking up a few groceries at the Bay, so we could make a picnic of it. It would be just like one of those old fashioned Massachusetts sleigh rides that Dick Dias and Woody Bartlett used to arrange when they all were attending the Hardy Grammar School in Beverly. The duffle bags would be even better for sitting on than hay, and if I didn't like the place we could come right back.

"How much is Ted charging?" I asked as innocently as possible.

"Just five dollars. . . ."

Then Brad stopped unbuttoning his dark red hunting jacket and really looked at me. His expression was so much like that of a little boy caught hiding a Christmas present that I had to laugh. After a doubtful moment, he joined in sheepishly.

"Okay," he admitted, "Dave and Ted sent me this morning to see Dudley Shaw, who's an old-time trapper. I went upriver with Dudley for a look. He'll. . . . He'd be our closest neighbor, about halfway between town and there. I think it's a windfall, Vena. But if you don't like it, we'll turn right around and come back."

"Six miles is a pretty long way," I hesitated.

"You're thinking of city miles. It won't seem that far here in the bush."

"I know," I put in so meaningly that he looked guilty all over again. "All right, we'll see. We've got to start living off the country, I know. Is there anything else I should be told, Brad?"

"I bought an air-tight heater and a folding table in town for six dollars," Brad said. "They're second hand but in good shape. We'll need them wherever we build. Some other odds and ends of furniture are already up there. Ted spoke of giving us some moose meat and some extra vegetables he has. Wouldn't take any money for them. . . . He's going to loan me a few tools, too. Oh, and I just now saw Dave. He'll set flour, baking powder, sugar, coffee, beans, oatmeal, sowbelly, molasses, raisins, tarpaper, coal oil, a lamp, Swede saw, heavy ax, stove pipe, and a few other things outside so Ted can get an early start."

"How much did the groceries cost?" I asked, wondering about our dwindling funds.

"Gosh, I don't know." Brad seemed embarrassed. "I was too excited to notice any prices when I was in the store this morning. Just now when I offered to pay for this grubstake Dave said he'd figure it out later and put it on our bill. So what could I say?"

Brad and Ted Boynton already had the sleigh packed when I went out into the chill blue of the following day. The woolens I wore made me feel awkward and bulky. The round man I'd seen the day before was ambling around the load, pulling at an occasional rope with short round fingers. The small yellow dog followed him importantly.

"Hello," the round man said, his oval face expanding into a friendly smile. When he touched his stocking cap, he took the opportunity of pushing a hank of black hair up under it. "You got something else to go on here? Get away from there, Bingo."

The little yellow dog, with a final sniff at my new boots, disappeared under the sleigh.

"Just this box of bread that Mrs. Ferguson baked for us, thanks, Ted," I said, and I lifted it to an empty place. "You've got pretty much of a load already, I guess."

"Yessum, but she'll do, Vena," Ted Boynton observed politely. "The trail isn't bad if we take our time. There's plenty of time, there is. The North has it all over cities when it comes to time. Say, now, that bread should taste pretty good when you get upriver. Mrs. Ferguson cooks mighty fine bread."

"Brad was telling me last night that you've got the reputation of being the best trail cook in the North," I noted somewhat overexpansively.

"Why now," Ted said, hitching up one strap of his faded blue overalls, "I've had fun cooking for the Harrimans and a lot of other millionaire dudes, anyway. Fun, cooking is. Like inventing, isn't it, particularly in the bush? You take a hurry-up pinch of this and a dab of that because the rest of the stuff ain't unpacked yet, and you wonder what you'll get. Mostly you think you know, but generally you don't. Isn't that about the way it is with trail cooking?"

"When it comes to cooking anywhere," I admitted, "I'm afraid my experience is pretty much limited to eating."

"Eating?" the round man exploded merrily. "There you are. You like to eat. Now where would us cooks be if there weren't those who like to eat? The only trouble I've found is that when someone likes eating enough, they usually aren't stumped for long when it comes to cooking. You won't have any trouble, I reckon. Everything set, Brad?"

Brad and I found seats on the duffle bags and waved to Mr. and Mrs. Ferguson who responded from the frosted window of the hotel. Ted Boynton, wedged comfortably up front, chirruped to the horses who started at a gallop. The little yellow dog ran in front of the team, barking menacingly at the dogs who appeared in the purplish shadows of log cabins we passed on our jingling way west out of Hudson Hope. After a short distance, the snow appeared unbroken except for snowshoe tracks.

The horses slowed to a walk, and Bingo scurried here and there in the bush after varying hares. About three miles beyond the settlement, we passed a cozy low cabin that Brad said was Dudley Shaw's. There was no telltale coil of wood smoke, though, to indicate that he was up yet. We continued on, through towering spruce and giant poplar now, up the trail that followed the high and almost level north bank of the Peace River which was now warmly honeyed by sunlight.

The three small log structures looked so forlorn that, with the sympathy of a kindred spirit, I knew we couldn't pass them by. They appeared suddenly when the two horses pulled around a stand of snow-ladened pines into a clearing that had been hewn out of the forest. A frozen stream wound through the opening to the edge of a cliff where, in what was now an incandescent tower of ice, it precipitated to the Peace River.

"Good water the year around," Ted noted, "comes from springs a few miles from here on Bullhead Mountain."

The cabin nearest the river seemed a trim rectangle, amber beneath the jade restfulness of blue spruce and lodgepole pine. My eyes traced the pleasant path one could take to dip the water pails in the brook. I gladdened at the space where a tiny garden spot could later be fenced against deer and moose.

"We're shot with luck," I heard Brad breathe to himself, but aloud he ventured hopefully, "Do you like it, Vena?"

By this time, I had followed a trail made by moose tracks to the buildings. My spirits started to fall as I examined more closely the one I'd been particularly admiring.

"Perfect," I was surprised to hear my husband murmur

Vena with .22.

Brad, waiting for game.

exultantly. He disregarded a drift to stand beside me. "Absolutely perfect."

"Hasn't the roof sort of given away in places?" I suggested timidly.

"Roof?" he echoed, face beaming. "It won't take us long to put up a good roof. I patched this one a bit yesterday with some old boards. See there? And just look at those spruce logs, will you? Did you ever see straighter, sounder logs?"

"But," I pointed dubiously, trying to evaluate the cabin by his standards, "aren't they kind of far apart in places?"

"That's because they were put up when green," he explained triumphantly, glancing toward Ted Boynton for confirmation.

"Flows the year around," called back Ted. "Never gets muddy like some of the muskeg brooks in this country."

"Anyway," Brad said, "they've dried out in fine shape now. They won't shrink and twist any more, not those logs. Cabins need rechinking every year or two, anyway. We can do it in a day with some moss and mud. You can see where I tightened that corner with moss. That's why I got home so late."

"The floor," I objected, indicating a portion that was not drifted with snow. "The floor is rotten."

"Floors are nothing," he scoffed. "They're even easier than chinking. We can lay a floor in a morning."

"With all that work," I noted with as little stiffness as I could manage, "we might as well build a new cabin."

"Certainly we're going to build a new cabin!" Brad seemed astonished.

"We are?" I inquired.

"You didn't think we were going to live permanently in these. . . . these shacks, did you?"

"Well, I kind of wondered."

"My gosh," Brad said. "No, we'll set up a makeshift camp in this one by the river if it's all right with you. Then we can begin tearing down those others for the materials in them. Well, isn't that about what Thoreau did? Didn't he write about buying James Collins' shanty for $4.25 and using the boards? We're getting these for nothing."

"I'm not disputing you," I said weakly. "You just frightened me, that's all."

He gave me a queer glance.

"If it's all right with you," he said carefully, "Ted and I will unpack. It is all right, isn't it, honey? We'll never find such a perfect place as this. And this way we won't have to wait until Spring to build. We can start right away."

We stood together two hours later, he and I, and watched Ted Boynton disappearing down the aisle among the trees. I'd never been in the woods before unless you counted vacations at Essex, a few miles from Boston, and in New Hampshire's White Mountains. Brad had hunted, fished, and camped throughout New England and southeastern Canada ever since his teens, but he'd never lived in the wilderness.

The horses, the creaking sleigh, the little yellow dog, and finally the swaying rotund shape vanished. Suddenly, we were pioneers.

CHAPTER FIVE

HOW SILENT THE NORTH?

Seasoned spruce logs exhuded a fragrant greeting as my husband lifted me across the threshold of our first, if temporary, wilderness home.

The clean resin-yellowed walls, now tentatively chinked with bristling sphagnum moss, warmed my heart toward the former owner. When I eased into a squeaking moosehide chair that had been left wired safely beyond the reach of sharp-toothed animals, I knew this prospector had valued comfort as well as seclusion. He had been thoughtful, too. The small cook stove had been left so well greased that only where water had streaked down the pipe was there any rust.

"Vena!" The delight in Brad's tone brought me to my feet. "Look at what I've found."

He held a candle so invitingly that I scorned to look twice at cobwebs. Boards creaked, as I scrambled through a trap door in the floor and down a short ladder. There, slab shelves rested on pegs that had been set in the pole walls of a thrifty excavation. Shadowy bins yawned darkly below them. The blackened wood about me was so odoriferous with the tarry odor of preservative, put there to combat moisture and insects, that it was like getting a whiff of a deserted Cape Ann wharf on a warm spring day.

"That gravel-puncher was certainly a good builder," Brad noted with admiration. "There's not a trace of dampness. Why don't we fix up this building later on as a cache? For a storage shack, that is?"

"What did he keep down here?" I asked curiously.

"Oh, vegetables, canned milk, preserves; anything that freezing would spoil." He squinted appraisingly into the screened end of a wooden shaft. "This is for ventilation. After airing the place out, we can keep it closed except during chinooks and warm weather. This cellar can be fixed so that frosts will never nip anything. Well, I'd better get working, again. We've got to finish getting ready for night."

The big heater brought from Hudson Hope shoved the cold back from a snug corner that had been walled from the rest of the cabin by our forest-green tarpaulin. Brad brought in armfuls of freshly split live birch somewhat to my surprise. I had not realized that green wood will burn. The oil in this made it blaze hotly.

There was no need to keep the cook stove going. We'd had dinner with Ted Boynton who, besides giving us a moose quarter and several bags of vegetables, had been thoughtful enough to tuck three fat venison steaks in his grub box for more immediate use. Each had seemed large enough for a roast when he had pan fried them without grease in his huge iron skillet. Yet even I, who'd been strictly a sandwich-and-milkshake luncheoner in the city, had finished mine to the last charred rarity. That had left for our supper the beef sandwiches and cake I found Mrs. Ferguson had thoughtfully tucked in the box along with her plump brown loaves of bread. It seemed especially cozy to eat them in the soft glow of a coal oil lamp.

After washing and wiping the stainless steel cups that had held our coffee, I scraped frost from the nearest window pane with a thumbnail. The broad arc of the Peace River was a gleaming platinum strip in the moonlight.

I stood there entranced, comparing the wild and limitless beauty with the bedraggled winter sedateness of the Charles River when I had glimpsed it less than two weeks before at the foot of Gloucester Street. How fine life would be, I thought, if the millions in Boston and other cities could at least visit uncontrived magnificences like this. On further consideration, which included memories of beer cans and broken glass and discarded tissues, I was doubtful. People would soon spoil them, I decided.

"Are you about ready to turn in?" my husband yawned, unclasping the black webbing that bound our eiderdowns. He unrolled the robes onto inflated air mattresses that bulged side by side on the floor. "Big day tomorrow."

"Coming," I said, hurrying to assist him.

It was my first night in sheer wilderness, in isolation so complete that my city-conditioned mind found difficulty in comprehending the roadless immensities that stretched for hundreds of square miles in nearly every direction. Brad and I knew from studying large-scale maps that a lost man could stray westward all the way to the Pacific over 300 miles away, and never encounter a single thoroughfare to the Outside. If he could manage to make his way northward to the very Pole, he'd encounter no escape route except the slender Alaska Highway. This might be crossed unnoticed in a storm or at night. Lost greenhorns have managed to accomplish the feat in bright sunlight on clear fair days.

Yet I found the sub-zero wind that engulfed the cabin almost comforting in its intensity. Puzzled, I decided the reaction must result from a sharpened appreciation at being so warm and sheltered in the midst of such savage grandeur. The soft and beckoning eiderdowns, instead of merely being something to be tolerated, proved to be the most luxurious beds I'd ever experienced. With the softly inflated mattresses easing every changing tangent of my body, the sensation was literally one of reclining on air. Lying on this floor did not bother me, either. Everything here, so far from human contamination, seemed undefiled and even antiseptic.

When Brad turned off the coal oil lamp, however, my apprehension returned. I found myself trying to maintain a wall of conversation against the shadowy forest that pressed in on every side.

I hadn't admitted even to myself how much I'd been dreading this initial night deep in the untenanted emptiness of what I had so often heard called the Silent North. The very name suggested a frightening void. Its implication was especially disturbing to someone who'd always gone to bed in the reassuring, if annoying, company of a city's million nocturnal sounds.

My husband's answers to now desperately contrived questions became terser and quieter. His steady breathing finally replaced even the briefest of responding grunts. I was alone with the night.

February wind, roaring through the narrow river canyon a half mile upstream, rattled a pane above my head. I listened involuntarily as breezes toyed with surging open stretches in the otherwise frozen river. A lodgepole pine raked the shakes overhead. Some small animal, fleet as the mink I'd seen at fur farms, scampered across the roof. A pair of whisper-winged owls hooo-hoo-hoo-hoooed back and forth across the blue-black forest. Some bird I'd never heard before called in the distance, like a moonbeam turned to sound.

Trees boomed, as what Brad had explained was freezing sap harmlessly burst their innermost fibers. Ceaselessly expanding and shifting ice cannonaded. What I took to be a coyote began yapping. Then I realized I had been intent for moments on a lone deep howl. It became joined in an echo-

ing, wildly thrilling chorus that brought Brad sitting up
beside me.

"Wolves," he breathed. "Big Siberians. We're lucky, hearing them so close the first night."

He cleared the nearest frosted window glass with a warm
palm, and we watched shadowy forms moving in single
file up the icy road of river. When they blurred out of sight
finally against the crouching shapes of bluffs, I lay back
relaxed.

"Why," I asked wonderingly, "why do people call this
the Silent North?"

"Well," he mused sleepily, although in his voice there
was an answering undertone of fulfillment, "maybe it's
because they stay too far south to know any better. Isn't
this real country, Vena? You are beginning to like it, aren't
you?"

His hand found mine.

"Sorry about coming?" he ventured.

I caught my breath. The suddenly revealed answer surprised even me.

"I'm only sorry that we put it off so long," I told him sincerely and almost immediately fell asleep.

CHAPTER SIX

A HOME FOR THE BUILDING

Something about hewing your own home out of the wilderness returns one close to the beginning of things. The instinctive hut-building ardor of a small boy is the proof. Our building project seized us with such enthusiasm that, except for somewhat reluctant periods of eating and sleeping, we worked almost steadily.

We started our first morning upriver to take apart two of the three deserted log structures. The third, which we temporarily occupied, we left for later renovation as a storehouse. Thoreau had similarly occupied himself one hundred years before, also borrowing tools for his task.

"It is difficult to begin without borrowing," he had explained. "Perhaps it is the most generous course thus to permit your fellowmen to have an interest in your enterprise."

Henry Thoreau had even borrowed an ax. That may have been all right in Concord, Massachusetts. Woodsmen here in the subarctic regard their axes as top priority necessities even more vital than matches. Viewpoints differ. Certain tribes of Eskimos, according to Gus Krossa who whaled in the Arctic Ocean before becoming a Peace River trapper, loan their wives more willingly than their snow knives—the

wide blade with which snow blocks are cut for igloos. Anyway, we bought our axes and borrowed from Ted Boynton
only a block and tackle and a wrecking bar.

The most advantageous way to use the available materials,
we decided after much drawing and planning, was by
building a cabin twenty feet long and twelve feet wide.
Thoreau's woodland home had been two-fifths smaller. But
then, Thoreau had been a bachelor.

When I wasn't helping Brad salvage boards, slabs, logs,
and hardware, I tested one potential site after another.
My procedure was one that will work anywhere. I did enjoy certain advantages, of course. Our dream house, being
small, was the easier to visualize. Furthermore, I was surprised to discover that a couplet I'd liked to mumble when
exploring the block of woods behind our Hyde Park home
with Eva Jackson could be actually true. Here I really was
monarch of all I surveyed; my right there was none to dis-
pute.

Four stakes joined by twine of the correct lengths made
an easily movable outline. I'd sink the pegs in the crusted
snow. Then, stepping inside the enclosure, I'd make believe
I was in our new home. There was where I'd prepare savory
venison ragouts. We'd eat them here by the view. From the
door at that end, one path would lead to the brook which
was our water system, while another would curve dis-
creetly in the opposite direction.

We finally discovered the most nearly perfect location.
It lay in an angle of brook and river, a few yards from where
the crystal trickle left the flat in its hundred foot plunge to
the Peace. I was immediately puzzled by another problem.
At this time of year, how could we set the corner stones
deeply enough so that they would not be moved by frosts?

"The prospectors who stampeded through here around
'98 on their way to the Yukon had a pretty good trick," Brad
mentioned.

"That," I quoted, "was somewhat before my time."

"It'll still work today," he grinned. "All we have to do is build some bonfires. This brush needs thinning out, anyway, so there'll be plenty of fuel handy. They'll thaw the ground as far down as we want to go."

Ledge proved to lie a foot beneath the surface, affording an ideal base. Numerous flat slabs of clay-ironstone were at hand from the previous building operations. We skidded them over on a logboggan, improvised one evening by setting the ends of three light boards in a slot sawed and then chiseled from a short poplar log. This made the sturdy, rounded front needed for hauling the toboggan-like contraption over the snow.

Brad fitted together the low foundations, while I gathered bulging sacks of caribou moss from beneath the light snow that dusted a spruce swamp behind the clearing. The stones, which had come from strata exposed by the brook's channel, were so even that they laid up without trouble. By the time I'd completed my task, Brad was back at his salvage operations, this time amassing usable shakes for the roof.

All the building operations went along so pleasantly that I could appreciate how Thoreau had felt when he asked, "Should we forever resign the pleasure of construction to the carpenter?"

The only difficulty I had, as a matter of fact, was in struggling to prepare three good meals daily. Even Brad wasn't much help when it came to bread. Mine just wouldn't rise.

Thoreau had extolled the merits of unleavened loaves, advocating Cato's classical recipe: "Wash your hands and trough well. Put the meal into the trough, add water gradually, and knead it thoroughly. When you have kneaded it well, mould it, and bake it under cover."

I tried that ancient Roman method in desperation. What resulted was better for the addition of salt, sugar, and lard. After several days of hardtack, however, I found it more palatable to settle for Thoreau's other estimation: "It was fit that I should live on rice, mainly."

It took only one misadventure to teach me not to stir rice while it is boiling. We liked it hot with heavy black molasses and milk. Fortunately for my pride and our nearly empty pocketbooks, our appetites had become so robust that almost everything tasted delicious.

There was excitement in the smell of freshly sawed wood, as Brad trimmed the old logs to their new lengths. What sticks he couldn't then drag easily to our building site, we rolled with the aid of poles that made stooping unnecessary. I was glad all over again that we wouldn't have to wait until spring to fell and peel building timbers.

Boards were stacked in a neat, dry pile. So were the better slabs. Spikes went into one box, straightened nails in another, while odds and ends such as hinges and staples clanked into a third. We chuckled at the difficulties Thoreau had experienced in rescuing similar hardware from the cabin he'd purchased and razed for materials.

"I was informed that neighbor Seeley, a Irishman, in the intervals of the carting, transferred the still tolerable, straight, and drivable nails and spikes to his pocket," Thoreau noted wryly, "and then stood when I came back to pass the time of day, and look freshly up, unconcerned, at the devastation; there being a dearth of work, as he said."

All was soon in readiness for actual building. We'd never considered ourselves able to afford a home while in the city. Here we were to have one in just a few days.

"And it won't keep us poor the rest of our lives, either," Brad noted with satisfaction.

"I still don't see how we're going to get those heavy logs in place?" I fretted. "Oh, the low ones won't be any trouble. But how about the high ones?"

"Nothing to it, Vena," he promised.

Anyone can build a good log cabin, my husband asserted, bolstering my morale and no doubt reinforcing his own at the same time. The job is not painstaking. There are not even any set and fixed rules to hold one in restraint. Constructing a warm, sturdy, and presentable log cabin is actually far less complicated than putting up a satisfactory frame dwelling.

After all, the wool-shirted pioneers who hewed the United States and Canada out of the North American forests had been for the most part inexperienced men, hadn't they? Hadn't they worked in a maximum of haste, moreover, with a minimum of tools? If there had been anything complex about log work, wouldn't they have turned to some other type of building? What could I say to such a man?

We lifted the two long sill logs into place without event, one end at a time. Then with even less effort we laid the first two short logs across them.

"How about fitting the corners?" I now worried. "That, well, it looks terribly difficult. Especially," I added, "with an ax."

Too many people today, Brad assured me—and, I suspect, himself—take an occasional wistful look at log cabin pictures and sadly vow that ax work is not for them. The happy fact, it seemed, is that no ax is required for the construction of a wilderness home. We could notch these sticks with a saw. His gaze strayed a bit doubtfully, as if that might not be a bad idea. Or we could do the job with a chisel and mallet. It may have been the expression on my face that made him grip the handle of his ax more tightly.

"An ax is quicker," he maintained stoutly. "Oh, I'm not just going to stand back and hack by eye. That's something for the movies. You don't cut a dress by guess work, do you? No, we'll measure and mark everything as we go along. That way, it's easy. Say, maybe I'll write a book about it some day."

When the bottom round had been leveled, squared, and then spiked firmly together at the corners, I strung moss liberally along the tops of the four logs to fill any crevices. Once the second round was in place, I tamped in more moss with a homemade mallet and a long chisel-like piece of wood that Brad called a spud. He had whittled it, with a four-inch blade at the end of a two-foot handle, from a piece of seasoned birch. Additional moss was strewn atop the latest four logs. The rising walls fairly bristled.

"We'll finish off that caulking later and plaster it with clay," Brad promised. "This way we can leave up to two inches between the logs, which will make it a lot easier to keep the cabin true."

Mythical log cabins in my girlhood reveries, when I had gotten over wanting to drive a fire truck and before my stage aspirations, had always fitted without a flaw. No wonder the task had seemed so unsurmountable when Brad had first dreamed aloud about building our own north woods abode!

The fact that logs are small at one end and large at the other had needlessly worried me. The way to compensate for this taper, it now seemed, was merely to alternate the direction of each round of four, so that the butt of each log would always lie above the top of the log directly below it. I still didn't understand.

"Look," Brad despaired, picking up four unused wooden matches, "here's the way it works."

He laid the four matches side by side with the heads all at one end. The match heads, wider as the log butts are wider, produced a fan-like effect. Then Brad moved the first and third matches, so that their heads lay in the opposite direction. I saw how a square-cornered rectangle was thus formed. I nodded a little crestfallenly. So it was as simple as all that!

My husband laid long pole skids up which to roll the next few logs. He pried at one end of each with short easy bites, using a light dry pole. I prevented that end from rolling back by means of a rope I kept snubbed, with almost no exertion on my part, around whatever tree was handiest. Then we'd tie up that extremity and shift to the other.

The block and tackle, suspended from a portable tripod, contrived by lashing the tops of thee poles together, made raising the upper logs an end at a time so easy that a couple of boys could have done it.

Spaces for the windows and door were sawed after the next to the last round of wall logs was in place. Brad, using a thin Swede blade, followed carefully measured and nailed guide boards which also served as temporary braces. When the plate logs went on, the walls were an adequate six feet high. It had taken only three days to raise them. The job had covered our hands with pitch which, as in Thoreau's case, imparted its fragrance to our meals.

The bright, warm days winged by simply and pleasantly. The back corner of an ax head was the only square Brad found necessary. A spike attached to a string was his plumb line. A discarded olive bottle, filled with contrasting tea, served as a level. Profiting from Thoreau's experience, we made no haste in our work but rather the most of it.

CHAPTER SEVEN

THE LATCH STRING

Whatever wind there is always lingers above the Peace River at dusk and again at daybreak, hesitating gently in the mellowness that softens this perceptible blending of the past and future.

The gale that had rattled shakes on the roof all night hushed now, charmed by the widening golden smile of the first morning of March. Laughter arose unimpeded from where surging open water was revealed by two rents in the river ice near the beckoning canyon a half-mile upstream. The sound blended pleasantly with the other noises of the new day.

"Happy," it seemed to gurgle, "happy."

A large pine slab which Brad was salvaging toppled with a ludicrous thump to the snow. The forest echoed with deep-throated enjoyment. A vagrant breeze, already fretful of the familiar patterns, whirled dislodged clay chinking after the wood in a gay festoon of dust. It moulded my woolen skirt briefly before quieting. A saw hummed, as my husband resumed work on the incomplete rectangle of a door. Then his hammer rang out cheerily. The river laughed harmoniously back.

47

"Happy," the current sang. "You're in the woods and happy, happy, happy."

The world still has room, I decided, for those who prefer the unimproved works of God to the civilized savagery of man-made cities. My mind turned almost ponderously toward the mass of discontented city men who complain idly of their hard lots when, as Thoreau noted, they might be improving them.

"What really is happiness?" I wondered aloud, as I stood there on the river bank and listened to my husband working.

Already the wind, having rested in the nick of eternity, was starting to blow again. It swept the laughter of rushing water ahead of it. When it romped around a corner of our nearly completed cabin, it caught up some of the fragrance of freshly notched logs. I breathed deeply.

"My dwelling was small, and I could hardly entertain an echo in it," Thoreau said. "But it seemed larger for being a single apartment and remote from neighbors."

That was our first thought when—now that walls had been bedded into place with surprising quickness, and in five more days the cabin had been roofed and floored—we needed only to hand the door before our home in the woods would be ready for occupancy.

Our second thought was price. Thoreau's itemized building expenses in 1845 totaled a thrifty $28.12. Roofing paper, transportation, air-tight heater, table, stove pipe, and incidentals brought our own costs to exactly $48.16.

Brad was bringing over the door now. I hurried to take one end of it, not so much because he needed any assistance as because I wanted to share in this finality. We fitted the portal, wedging penny-thin chips around it to assure proper clearance. Then I held it, while Brad screwed fast the hinges.

"Try it," he authorized at last, letting out his breath.

"Uummm, not bad. I'll just shave this corner down a bit with my knife. There, that should do it. Fine. Now for the latch."

Brad had already spent several evenings whittling two heavy birch catches. One of these was already attached to the door. The other was screwed to the door frame. One extremity of a beautiful hand-fashioned latch, consisting of a twenty-inch length of birch, had been bolted to the door in such a way that the piece lifted freely in an arc. Resting across the door in the two narrow openings thus presented, it served as a movable bar.

Brad tied a rawhide thong to the latch with one of his knots which, although far less involved than mine, always seem to behave the way they're supposed to. We both went outdoors. He shoved the free end of the thong through a spike hole he'd made near the edge of the door a few inches above the catch. Then he disappeared back inside the cabin, shutting the door behind him.

"Go ahead and try it," came his muffled voice.

I considered the closed barrier a moment. I decided to knock. My knuckles tapped in a way I took to be polite.

"Come in," responded a haughty voice after a carefully timed moment. "I'll see if the master is at home."

A rush of air swayed the latch string away from my outstretched fingers. Brad's second invitation was less formal than assertive. Even more urgent was the third which also wore some of the timbre of an entreaty. I finally captured the thong and pulled. The door, unbarred, opened violently under the pressure of wind. There was a loud bang.

"Ouch," my husband gasped, rubbing his head.

"Oh, did it hurt?" I tried to ask with the proper anxiety.

"Humph," he grunted finally. "How could it hurt, getting hit on the head by a door?"

A titter escaped me.

"So," he stated with a not entirely respectful pat, "you think it's funny, do you, whacking your poor husband on the cranium?"

He made a playful grab for me. Squealing, I ducked under his arms. When he did catch me, his reaction was no more disrespectful, but it was evidenced with a more resounding quality. Then he began to chuckle, too. We both laughed so unrestrainedly that soon we just sprawled limp and breathless on the new floor.

"At least," Brad gasped finally, "the cabin is officially dedicated. Instead of breaking a bottle of champagne, we used my head. Much more economical, considering the state of our finances. . . ."

We leaned weakly against the north wall and admired the panorama afforded by the line of four double windows, banked overlooking the Peace River in the long south side of the cabin.

"This way," I noted with increasing appreciation, "we will enjoy all the sunshine there is in winter, won't we? And the view. . . . Was there ever such a view?"

Before us glittered nearly a mile of the wilderness stream whose waters flow from west to east through the entire backbone of the Rocky Mountains, hesitate in Great Slave Lake, and finally surge northward to mingle with the Arctic Ocean at Coronation Gulf.

Brownish yellow shale cliffs, as high as the one on which the cabin stood, lifted from the opposite shore. Above these an unbroken line of hills, dark with spruce, extended a sheltering arm that eventually curved out of sight upriver beyond the narrow rocky canyon that had beckoned us since our arrival.

" 'I intend to build me a house which will surpass any on the main street in grandeur and luxury, as soon as it pleases me as much,' " I quoted, " 'and will cost no more than my present one.' "

"Well, Thoreau has certainly been right so far," Brad agreed. "We've proved the first part of our dream. I'd say we've earned a vacation. Let's do something we've hankered to ever since arriving here."

My eyes followed his upstream.

"Sure," he grinned. "Let's follow the Peace up into the mountains. We'll have plenty of stormy days later on to put this place in order. Get on your ski clothes if you want. I'll pack a lunch. Let's find out what lies the other side of Box Canyon."

CHAPTER EIGHT

RIVER CANYON

Shale and dusty clay piled about our boots as, with giant steps, we descended to the river by the only route for a half mile on either side of the cabin that could be safely followed without ropes. The snow on our flat a hundred feet above the Peace was still too deep for comfortable walking. Along the river's rim, however, was a smooth icy sidewalk where overflow had frozen.

Winters don't close the North, as we were already discovering. They open it, rather, providing congealed highways that twine enticingly into otherwise inaccessible country. For those on showshoes, the snow carpets the deep tangles of deadfalls that clog too often burned stretches of subarctic wilderness.

"Nice?" Brad asked, falling into step beside me.

"Uummm, nice," I agreed.

The air above had been tempered by a raw wind. On this cliff-sheltered expanse of river, the sun made itself felt. Squinting, I found myself fumbling to unbutton my mackinaw with one hand while groping for sun glasses with the other. The greenish lens gave the dazzling world an agreeably cool aspect, although I could see heat waves shimmering above the ice. They bent downriver, giving what breeze there was the semblance of being visible.

"What are those things up on the cliffs that look like hornet nests?" I wondered.

"Cliff swallow homes," Brad replied. "Dudley Shaw was telling me about them. Thousands will be colonizing just below the cabin by Spring."

Then I saw the huge prints. The size of soup plates, they were about eighteen inches apart in practically a straight line. The numerous coyote tracks, that veered and circled inquisitively, seemed tiny by comparison. So did the neat dog-like progress of a fox, characterized by the way its heavy tail had brushed the snow.

It hadn't stormed since we had arrived. Old and fresh game trails were everywhere. What were these tremendous marks? Those wolves we had heard the first night? But we'd seen a pack of them, and no imprints similar to this single line were anywhere.

Brad was looking at me as if expecting a question. I forced my lips tightly together. We rounded the bend that led into the slit called Box Canyon. I was amazed. What had appeared to be one track now branched into no less than five different trails.

"Yes, it's those same wolves," Brad smiled. "Dudley was telling me they sometimes travel in single file that way in snow, one putting his feet exactly in the prints of the wolf ahead."

We were now in the chasm where the Peace River narrows between overhanging rock walls, less than the length of a football field apart in one place. A wind blustered out of the shadows whose realm this was. I shoved the glasses up on my forehead and buttoned my coat.

"Magnificent," my husband breathed.

It was, in a stark and primitive way more impressive

than any gently contrived beauty. I followed his gaze up an acute slope to our left that slanted precipitously skyward for what must be a thousand feet. A flutter of dust high above caught my attention. I felt Brad's arm strong around me as, somewhere in the murkiness ahead, rock fell with a rumbling echo. Dark blotches on either side of the icy passage indicated that this was no uncommon occurrence.

"We'd better walk along the middle of the river," Brad suggested. "The ice is pretty much of a jumble there, isn't it? Doggone, the snow's plenty deeper, too. Well, we've got plenty of time."

We built our fire where the north bank benched down to meet the river which had again widened into a sunlit expanse. Alexander Mackenzie, who after explorers had failed for 301 years became the first man ever to cross the North American continent above Mexico, had camped nearby in 1793 on his epic journey to the Pacific.

There are two reasonably sure ways to tell if a man is a cheechako, even if you've never seen him, merely by glancing at the evidence of his fire. Tenderfeet here as everywhere waste time and energy on bonfires which, scorching anyone who ventures close enough for warmth, defeat their own purpose. Too, newcomers to the cold climes habitually build fires against a reflective surface instead of placing themselves between the flames and reflector. Brad had never lived in the woods before nor had he ever been in the subarctic. Because he had camped in extreme weather along both sides of the Atlantic end of the Canadian border since school days, however, he made neither of those mistakes.

"Did an emperor ever have a finer banquet table?" he asked now, clearing snow with his boot away from a half circle of boulders. "What say we get the fire going out front here? Then we can sit in among those rocks, so they'll throw the heat on our backs. Why not strip some of the lower branches off those young spruce? They'll make a fine seat."

Reaching into the game pocket of his hunting coat, he took out a yellow waterproofed bag containing the lunch. He put two stainless steel cups, a boiling kettle which consisted of a large tomato can to which a wire bail had been attached through a pair of nail holes, and four small packages on a nearby sandstone slab already the more interesting because ripples of the ancient beach from which it had been hardened corrugated its yellow surface.

"Uummm," I sighed in anticipation. "When are we going to light the fire?"

"We have to get the tinder first," he smiled. "Want to take your first lesson on outdoor fires? All right, birch bark is good to start one with. The oil in it makes it burn under almost any condition, even when it's dripping wet. There's no need to cut the tree, either. We can pull off all we need without disfiguring anything."

He gave a satisfied nod after we'd stripped off several handfuls of loose chalky bark.

"Now let's break off some of those dead twigs in the underneath parts of these spruce," he said. "They're full of oil, too. They're fine to start a fire with by themselves, as a matter of fact."

He dropped the birch bark in a tiny heap. The dry spruce he spread loosely on top.

"Now do we light the fire?" I asked, reaching for one of the two waterproof and unbreakable match containers I had been given strict orders always to carry on different parts of my person, just in case.

"Not yet," Brad replied. "What we have there would flash up and be ashes in a minute. We need some real fuel. That fallen poplar jutting over the bank is the thing."

We broke dry branches off the upper part of the deadfall. Brad angled the smaller of these in a kind of wigwam over the birch bark and spruce.

"See how I'm leaving plenty of space for ventilation," he pointed out. "When these catch, we can pile on the heavier stuff."

"When do we light it?"

"Soon," he smiled.

A long green pole was angled between two stones to hold the boiling kettle. This Brad filled high with icicles and hung in place. I unscrewed the metal top of a match case.

Shaking his head, Brad cut two green willow wands. On each he skewered about a dozen walnut-size tidbits of moose meat which he had sliced from the remains of the forequarter Ted Boynton had given us. These he had already covered liberally with salt and pepper before wrapping in wax paper. He laid the two spits carefully to one side, then selected and peeled a poplar sapling twice as thick as a broom handle. He leaned this near where the fire was to burn.

"Now, Vena," he nodded.

My fingers were so unsteady that I broke the first match. The second burst into pink prongs against the rough side of the holder. Shielding the flame with my crouched body, I applied it cautiously to the birch bark. Sweet black smoke filled my nostrils. The white strips, curling and bubbling, became alive with dancing combustion. Here in this wilderness it was easy to understand why fire had been regarded along with air, earth, and water as one of the four elements. The spruce ignited with a crackling and snapping. Before both had flared to greyness, the poplar was burning hotly and quietly.

"Perfect," my husband beamed. "Now for the kabobs."

A meat-ladened rod in each hand, I thrust the juicy red tidbits into clear flame to sear them. Then I held them to one side and, twisting the sticks, roasted the meat slowly.

Brad had already added a half cup of icy water to a previously mixed cup of flour, teaspoon of baking powder, teaspoon of salt, tablespoon of butter, and handful of raisins. He worked the dough quickly, so that as little as possible of the leavening gas would escape. He soon had a ribbon some three inches wide. This he wound around the peeled stick, the sap of which had been sputtering in the heat.

"Bannock," Brad explained, allowing the twisted dough to brown gradually over a glowing mass of coals. "You'd better drop a few more icicles in that can if you will please, Vena. That should give us enough water for tea. Here, let me hold those kabobs for you."

Broken into steaming pieces and dripping with butter, the bannock tasted better than the finest biscuit I could remember. Never had meat been so tender and delicious as the kabobs, bitten directly from the willow spit while still sizzling from the embers. The vapor that hovered above the cups of black tea was in such a plane of sunlight that it resolved into two swirling greenish curls, tinged regally with scarlet.

Brad laid some long heavy chunks of poplar at right angles to us across the cherry-red coals. Warm and sated, I lounged contentedly back and watched flame curl around them. Lazily we contemplated the bright snow cones of the Rockies that thrust into the incredible blueness one sometimes glimpses on the desert but which attains its most startling magnificence in the frigid dry reaches of the world. Such beauty, I thought, must be reserved as a special reward for those who venture into distant, deserted places.

The nearby fire, the sun, and aroma of spruce and poplar, and the wild free whine of wind high above had a soothing effect. Reaching an arm around me, Brad closed his eyes with a satisfied sigh. The last I remembered was a deep wonder at how my senses, no longer chained by the routine of a city existence, found soul-tingling excitement in the everyday functions of sky, earth, and spirit.

"Shams and delusions are esteemed for soundest truths,

while reality is fabulous." Had Thoreau ever said anything truer? "If men would observe realities only, and not allow themselves to be deluded, life would be like a fairy tale."

A voice prodded at me. It seemed as far away as the wolfish breeze which scooped up mouthfuls of snow from the peaks, giving to the almost unreal scene a sense of vitality that the rumble of a slide confirmed. The tones interfered with the pictures that still drifted agreeably just beyond the fringe of my consciousness. I tried not to listen, attempting with almost perceptible effort to shrink from the distraction that worried my shoulder.

"Wake up, Vena."

The pictures were almost gone now. Curious impressions hurtled after them; a gale-tormented emptiness heaving with wind, the steep dusty descent by which we had reached the river, footsteps crunching in snow that was still deep away from the icy overflow, and the curious bleak rattling of frozen leaves. Then I sensed, in their place, the nearby snapping of our campfire. I heard the dog-like howling of wind that no longer romped high in the hills but poked its cold nose among the rocks by the river bottom.

"Wake up, sweet," Brad was urging, and I clung to him speechlessly for a moment until I could fend for myself in this wide-awake world. "We should have started back an hour ago."

All that remained of sunlight, I realized, was a rosy swath on a high spruce ridge across the river. The pistol reports of trees, whose sap was congealing, signified that night cold was moving in.

Ice boomed on the Peace River, as we started back into a boisterous wind toward the shale bank we must ascend to reach the cabin. Gusts blew now out of the northeast. I saw a thin crack shoot like lightning across a glassy expanse swept clear of snow. We were in Box Canyon again. Even though Brad had said the ice here must be at least twelve feet thick, the sight gave me a funny feeling.

The very whiteness of the ice made it seem brittle, although I remembered from skating days that it's the darkest ice which is the youngest. Black, blue, green, and even dark grey ice may be unsafe. When there is any danger, I recalled dully, it is well to carry a long pole. Then if one breaks through, the pole can act as a bridge by whose support one may be able to clamber to safety. I turned that recollection over in my mind as, with the eastern end of the narrow gorge brightening before us, Brad started to ease over to the near side. Wind sweeping up the wide channel ahead blasted at us.

"Our eiderdowns will feel snug tonight, won't they?" I asked, shielding my eyes from a cloud of dust snatched up by the gale.

"Sure will, even if I haven't got around to building those bunks yet."

As the air currents were snatching at hjs words, I heard a thunder. The thud of falling shapes resounded in my ears. Something hurled me into the cold snow. I tried to squirm away, but whatever it had been now covered me. Then I heard a gasp. Whatever shielded me went limp for a long moment. When I managed to twist free, I saw it was Brad.

"Get back," he was ordering between clinched teeth. "Back."

He was trying to get up as he scrambled toward mid-ice, but one leg would not behave. I struggled to help him despite his orders. The snow behind us was ugly with shale whose descent from the rock walls above was still marked by a trickle of dust.

Not until we were yards away from danger did I think to stop tugging. Brad worked himself around until he was in sitting position. His face became even whiter as he felt his leg. When we looked at it, nothing seemed broken, but the knee was already swollen and discolored. Then he again tried to stand. I felt the sudden drag of his weight.

"Guess there's no cabin for me tonight," he said at last, forcing a grimace into a smile. "I'll be okay camping out, though. You get on back while it's light."

"I'll help you all I can," I guess I said.

"No good," he gritted. "It's too cold to be hobbling along in the face of this wind. Besides, it would be pretty rough making it up that bank at night, and there's no shelter around there. Oh, we could make it, but it wouldn't be good sense.

Something seemed expected of me, so I nodded.

"You get a move on before it's too dark, Vena. You can't miss your way. It'll be easy for me to get in by daylight to-morrow. . . . Well, why are you waiting?"

"I'm not waiting," I explained patiently, biting my cheek so that my voice would remain steady. "I. . . . I'm staying."

CHAPTER NINE

THE WHITE WIND

The wind that earlier that day had frolicked high in the mountains now howled upriver in a frigid surging mass that seemed almost visible. Trees snapped in rebellion against the frost. Ice boomed.

"I'm staying," I declared, keeping my teeth sharp against my cheek.

My husband was hunched on the snow that in the narrowness of Box Canyon thickly frosted the ice of the Peace River. He massaged the leg that stretched helplessly in front of him, and he glared. I returned the look, trying to keep tears from my eyes.

"I am staying," I guess I blurted. "I am, Brad."

"Come here, honey," he said finally. When I didn't move, I guess he tried to haul himself toward me. "Come here, Vena. Sure, you can stay."

He somehow had me by the sleeve now, drawing me into the warm security of his arms.

"Don't rub your eyes. It isn't good for them. "Besides . . ." He was having trouble with his own voice. "Besides, everything's all right. My leg is okay. I just sort of retwisted an old football knee I got at Kimball Union Academy. I could get back tonight if we had to. But you just wait and see what a comfortable camp we can fix."

"Won't it be pretty cold here in the canyon?" I asked.

"Who's staying in the canyon?" he asked, laughing as if I'd tried to be funny. "We're going back to where we had that fire. That's only a few hundred yards. Always remember this, Vena. The wilderness is the friendliest place in the world if instead of fighting it one just takes advantage of what it freely offers. We'll make out fine."

I was thankful the wind was at our backs, as I helped Brad upriver. Finally, in the blue northern twilight, we saw where the land slanted down to the level of the ice.

"It's getting pretty dark down here," my husband noted. "There's our spot up ahead there to the right. I'll be able to make it alone if I take my time. We'll need a lot of firewood."

I started to protest.

"See that small, forked birch on that shelf?" Brad interrupted. He unsnapped the leather guard from around his sheath knife and extended the whitish staghorn handle toward me. "It should make a pretty decent crutch."

He watched me until I returned, trailing the stunted tree.

"Thanks," he said, and he trimmed away the branches before testing it. "That'll do fine. Now do you suppose you can go on ahead? We're going to need enough fuel to last the night."

I suppose I nodded, for he went on talking, the wind snatching at his words.

"Drag in all the dead wood you can find. It'll have to be dead because we haven't any ax. If it's off the ground, so much the better. Don't bother with birch. It's generally rotten when dead. Spruce and pine shoot off too many sparks. Poplar is best. Some cottonwood will do because it'll hold the fire. Bring in sections as large as you can easily manage. The fire will burn them to size easier than we can break them. I'll be along to help as soon as I can."

I hesitated in my task from time to time to watch his progress up the ice. Once when the crutch slipped, I ran toward him. Brad waved me back. Sky, mountains, and river quieted into deeper shades of blue. The air stilled as if to contemplate; imponderably, harmoniously, serenely. Again day, the past, was blending with the future night.

"There was never yet such a storm," I remembered Thoreau saying, "but it was music to a healthy ear."

Pausing to regain my breath, I realized I was no longer bothered with doubts. No one badly injured could be moving with as much agility. Already Brad, by the remains of the afternoon fire, had uncovered some huge twisted shapes of driftwood. I felt warm and tingling, as he praised the heap of fuel I was accumulating. Somewhere an animal howled.

"There's our reflector," Brad explained, as I helped him drag several stumps close behind the leaping blaze. "They'll throw the heat into our lean-to."

"What lean-to?" I asked.

"This one," he chuckled, balancing himself on the crutch. "Watch."

The thick matting of evergreen boughs on which we had lounged earlier that day still formed a soft flooring among the semi-circle of protecting boulders. He stripped branches from nearby spruce and made the resilient layer even thicker.

"That's our mattress," he grinned, as I heaped additional boughs for his use. "Now for the walls and ceiling."

He filled the spaces between the rocks with conifer limbs against which, taking his cue, I heaped snow. Three small spruce trees, laid across the rocks and reinforced with boughs, made a rustic ceiling. Sinking finally on the aromatic bed within the shelter, I felt muscles relaxing under the cheery insistence of the heat.

Flames roared up brightly, as Brad laid several long sticks

parallel to the opening. He placed the ice-filled tea pail within reach before edging beside me. I leaned forward to aid him when he started to unlace the boot on his injured leg, but he smiled, "Thanks. Better let me ease this off myself." I sank back again.

The wind was rising outside, but the living warmth of the blaze was all around. The gale seemed to be whirling splinters of ice from stars that blinked in the blue night sky. I closed my eyes to rest them.

"Nothing broken," I heard someone sigh in a faraway voice. "That's lucky."

I tried to open my lids. The effort was too great. I must have fallen asleep because when I did open them, the fire had burned to embers. I groped carefully for the wood pile and tossed some sticks into the coals. The dry poplar flared up quickly, flicking light through the lean-to and vitalizing it with fresh heat. I sat upright. Brad had disappeared. I was alone in the shelter.

Suddenly I realized I could no longer see the stars. Had all this been a dream, I wondered? But, no, I could still feel yielding browse beneath and smell its spicy fragrance. Trees banged occasionally. The river ice, although it now sounded subdued, was continuing its restless shifting. Then as I started forward, I felt a cold feather on my face, and another and another.

"Snowing," Brad said briefly, appearing out of the shadows. "Looks like a real storm. We'd better get moving."

"Your knee. . . ?"

"I've just been trying it out," he grimaced, easing in beside me. "It's pretty stiff, wrapped up the way I have it, but I can get along all right. What say we have a spot of this hot tea before setting out? You missed getting your share last night."

By the time we reached Box Canyon, snow was funneling through it with the suffocating whiteness with which smoke

The cabin in summer.

The cabin in winter.

envelops a train in a tunnel. There are never any blizzards
in the part of the North where we live, but the wind shriek-
ing along this narrow shadowy gorge gave that effect. Visa-
bility for the moment was blotted out as effectively as if we
were being smothered in raw cotton.

"Here." His voice seemed a trillion light years away, but
his arm was warm and near. "Let's keep out in the middle
even if the going is more rugged. Just take it easy, and I'll
be all right. There's no need to try to help. I'm doing fine.
I'll just keep an arm around you in case I stumble." There
was a silence. "Say, isn't this something!"

He sounded enthusiastic, even though the white wind
assaulted the words with stinging fervor, whirling them
away almost before they could reach my ears. The universe
seemed to be heaving with tempest. There was nothing to do
but cling to one another and to plod forwards, step by step.
I recollected, of all things, how the iron-fenced whiteness of
Boston Garden loomed chaste and beckoning during evening snowfalls. I was a long, long way from Beacon Street.

The climb up the shifting, slipping cutbank was what I'd
been dreading most. Even that wasn't too bad, although
Brad had to inch up part of it in a sitting position. Balancing
became precarious when he left the shale. We sidled across
the hard brittle steepness that lay between the loose rock
and the depression in the bank through which, grasping a
clump of wolf willow, we were finally able to haul ourselves
onto the level land above.

Ahead, through the whiteness of flakes that sifted with
little bursts of sound into the bush, our cabin beckoned. We
furrowed toward it. My fingers caught stiffly at the wel-
coming latch string. There was the squeak of hinges and
then the hollow bang of the slab door, as a gust swung it
inward. Snow, wind, and fresh cold followed us into the
quiet fragrant chill of our forest abode.

"Home!" I'd envisioned myself trilling the word rapturously, so I was a little horrified at the croak I emitted. "We made it."

Brad gave me a surprised glance.

"Sure," he said. "Do you want to get some water while I get the fire going?"

We had fallen into the northern custom of leaving fuzz sticks, kindling, and dry wood ready by the stoves. Brad was piling the former carefully in the air-tight heater as I went out with the two pails, taking the ax from beside the door as I passed. The storm seemed different now. It was just an ordinary fall of snow, and I was merely taking an ordinary stroll to the brook for water; only this time I did saunter somewhat faster than usual.

Brad was already adding heavy wood to the small cluster of pronging flame when I returned, exhilarated and breathless. The single room, although as frigid as ever, seemed the warmer for the smell of heat. Fuzz sticks, I described to myself inconsequently, are made by slicing down a preferably straight grained piece of softwood kindling several dozen times without detaching any of the curling shavings. The secret, I repeated mentally, is to let the blade drag behind the hand instead of trying to hold it at right angles to the wood. At the end of the stroke, a slight twist of the wrist will bend the shaving out of the way.

Indians, Brad had noticed, whittled toward themselves, claiming this gives one better control of the knife. The white men he knew continued to whittle fuzz sticks away from themselves, however, perhaps because of subconscious adherence to long preached safety rules. The backwoods substitutes for paper were blazing fervently as I set down the filled buckets, and the heavier fuel was catching, too.

"How's about a steaming bowl of oatmeal, chock-full of plump sweet raisins?" Brad suggested. "We can make it right here on the heater. Instead of cooling it with milk, what say we let big yellow blobs of butter melt over it instead?"

"Uummm," I enthused. "Here, let me do it."

"All right," he grinned. "And coffee, Vena? I've been dreaming about the smell of coffee. Let's forget about that percolator contraption. Let's just use the pot itself, and that clean fresh brook water, and a big tablespoon of grounds for each cup and another for the pot. . . ."

"I'll make it," I interrupted. "Why don't you lie down and rest your leg?"

"All right, you make it," he acquiesced again, "but I'd rather sit here where I can enjoy the fire. Don't stir those grains, honey. Just let them float. No, better set it back a little further. I'll keep an eye on it. When it starts to boil, it's done. Maybe we'll even plunge in a burning stick bushwhacker-style to settle the grounds."

The fire crackled reassuringly, shoving back the frost. Wind, fresh from the Arctic Circle eleven degrees farther north, swirled around our new log home. Already the storm seemed immeasurable light years away. I silently thanked the Almighty for the commonplace things about us that suddenly meant so much.

"The necessaries of life are food, shelter, clothing, and fuel," Thoreau had said. To these requirements I added the one spice that could make them savory; mutual love! Here in northern British Columbia, I knew Brad needed me as surely as I required him. The realization gave me a warm satisfaction of belonging.

"What is happiness?" I wondered aloud for the second time in two days.

"Dunno," he responded. "Having what you need and being contented with it, I guess."

"That must be why I'm so happy now," I decided, dropping down beside his chair. "We do have everything we need, don't we, including each other!"

CHAPTER TEN

THE FARTHER PLACES

The happiest man we know lives in a log cabin, three miles from the nearest settlement and a similar distance from his closest neighbor, on the sunny bank of the Peace Rvier in northern British Columbia.

Years ago, a cabinet maker's apprentice in an English city, Dudley Shaw used to trudge several miles after work most evenings for a few free minutes of fishing. He came to his decision one dusk. When unspoiled spaces beckoned, why should he waste the vigorous years of his life merely snatching at fragmentary pleasure?

In his present spruce castle in the Canadian Rockies, what is he but a king? He runs a short trap line in winter to give him the odd $200 he needs to live royally another year. He is past 70, but there is a youthfulness in his step and a zest in his smile that are lacking in many a city man of 30. Whereas the latter often only exists, our friend lives—breathing clean air, beholden to none, doing what he wants to do most and giving it his best.

For several delightful weeks now, we had been those closest neighbors. I would have wondered at his happiness once. Even this particular March morning it might have left me somewhat dubious, if I had known Dudley then.

A stream of cool air trickled pleasantly between my shoulder blades, as I hunched up on one elbow in the gossamer lightness of my eiderdown. The cabin was redolent with spruce. I couldn't remember ever having slept more wonderfully.

Through the four windows in the south wall of our wilderness home I could see trees, mountains, and river marked by varying shades of blue. Snow still chalked the amethyst scene with gentle flakes. Some noise, or the dream of one, had aroused me. Now I stayed awake to wonder at the beauty of the approaching dawn.

The rhythm of Brad's steady breathing came pleasantly across the few feet of space that separated us. Wind puffed down the stove pipe. A coyote yipped. The hooo-ho-ho-hooo of an owl had a beauty whose loneliness was dispelled by the deeper echoing answer of her mate. I wished someone were awake to share all this with me.

"Brad," I called in the faintest possible whisper.

Darkness seemed to bulge deeper than ever within the log house when the syllable drifted away unanswered. If he were really asleep, I told myself, it would probably be better not to arouse him. Twenty-four hours ago, I'd been worrying about getting back to the cabin. That had not proved too difficult. It had been harder to keep him off the injured leg afterward. I heard myself sigh. Husbands are difficult sometimes. I turned to look again at the approaching day.

"When I took up my abode in the woods, every morning was a cheerful invitation to make my life of equal simplicity with Nature," Thoreau had written, and a century later we were finding it that way, too. "The morning is the most memorable season of the day. For an hour, at least, some part of us awakes which slumbers all the rest of the day and night."

How many of my friends, I admitted ruefully, were equipped by experience to agree with that philosophy.

When I'd lived in cities, the words wouldn't have held any meaning that I could have appreciated. Most of my contacts with dawn had been from the going-to-bed end. Then the empty streets had been damper, chillier, and even more oppressing than usual. I suspect Thoreau must have been thinking of inhabitants of cities when he remarked, "Some would find fault with the morning red, if they got up early enough."

All these thoughts floated across my mind with the almost hypnotic clarity with which one's mental processes drift unimpeded when the electric currents of the brain first commence their reversal from sleep to refreshed consciousness. Each new impression was as if a page had been turned. Now I was concerned with Thoreau again. I was remembering the medicine he recommended to keep us well, serene, and contented.

"For my panacea, let me have a draught of undiluted morning air," he begged whimsically. "If men will not drink this at the fountainhead of day, then we must even bottle and sell it for the benefit of those who have lost their subscription tickets to morning time. But remember, it will not keep quite to noontime even in the coolest cellar."

It was then I saw the shadow. It flitted noiselessly and shapelessly across the log wall beside me where brightening dawn, smiling through the bank of windows, made four frosty patches.

"Brad," I heard myself hiss in a small, tight voice.

"H'm," my husband yawned. "What?"

"I just saw. . . ." My throat seemed to shrink. "Brad, look . . . going down the path!"

He sat upright.

"Hey," he shouted surprisingly. "Hey, Dudley. Come on in. The latch string's out."

There was a silence broken only by the rustle of snow

brushing against the cabin and the echoing crack of ice somewhere along the river below. Then the wooden latch scraped free of its catch and rattled loosely. The weight of the slab door made the hinges creak. Fresh air fluttered some loose papers on a shelf, and one of them fluttered to the floor.

A stranger stood indecisively in the sapphire angle revealed by the half opened door. What I had taken to be the wings of some frightening, misshapened bird proved to be snowshoes. Angled as they were over one shoulder, they looked huge and shadowy in the dimness.

"Come along in, Dudley," Brad invited heartily. "We were just about to have breakfast."

"Look who's talking," I thought.

The stranger was peering through thick-lensed glasses that sparkled in the light from the windows. He moved closer now, closing the door behind him. I could see that he was a small man, wearing an apparently brown woolen jacket that appeared shrunken and woolen trousers that seemed too tight. The reason, I soon learned, was not that his clothing was too snug but that in winter he wore two of everything. It's a much more effective way for an active individual to keep warm and dry, we discovered for ourselves, than the practice of changing to heavy burdensome winter garments.

"Ho, there," greeted the newcomer in a friendly voice that was not at all small. "Cheery cabin you have here. I was prowling by on my trapline and thought I'd check to see if you were bogged down. Had a message, too. You're doing noble, I see."

"Vena, this is Dudley Shaw," Brad introduced, starting to unsnap his eiderdown. "He bakes the best bread in Hudson Hope, even the women say."

"Oh, will you teach me how?" I asked.

"I don't know about that," Dudley admitted cautiously,

"It generally takes time to get the knack. But I'll be glad to tell you whatever I know, though. Main thing with bread is to keep on the offensive."

He looked at the birch crutch but didn't say anything about it.

"Thanks, I've already had breakfast," went on the visitor. "It'll cheer me up vastly to have some hot lap with you later, though, and powwow a bit. Got to look at a couple of traps above here. Then I'll stagger back this way."

"What does he mean by 'lap'?" I asked Brad curiously, hurrying to get into my clothes before the return of our nearest neighbor.

"Tea," Brad explained, proceeding with the ritual of fire making. "Dave Cuthill, down at Hudson's Bay, was telling me that Deadly has a vocabulary all his own."

"Deadly?" I said, shifting from one bare foot to another on the cold floor. "I thought his name was Dudley?"

"Actually, it's neither one," Brad replied, regulating the drafts so that the fire took on a deep-throated roar. "Actually, it's Reginald. Dave was telling me about it."

The whole matter seemed confused at first. As a matter of fact, the pattern is characteristic of any frontier country. At least half the sourdoughs we later came to know had acquired apparently ordinary cognomens that were totally unrelated to their own. King Gething, who operates a coal mine a few miles west of us on Bullhead Mountain, is actually Quentin Franklin Gething. Joe Barkley, who freights winters between Hudson Hope and the Graham River for trader Teddy Green (Edward not Theodore), if not Joseph at all but. . . . Well, Clara, his wife, says Joe would rather forget that. The way Dudley became connected with his identification is an example of how such things happen in the north.

When Reginald W. Shaw was a cheechako—a green tenderfoot, as contrasted to the sourdough who has spent at least one winter in the subarctic—he was looking for some summer work at a now deserted camp up Portage Creek several miles north of us. A mining company was sinking a shaft there in an effort to discover an old gold-clogged channel. They didn't succeed, incidentally, probably because the depression that looks as if it might be a filled-in river bed is just a furrow left by a melting glacier.

"Come and get it," the cook dared, banging warningly on a galvanized tub. "Come and get it, or I'll throw it away."

Young Shaw, although he was packing a lunch, was invited to eat as is the custom. This particular backwoods chef prepared his meals along the familiar BBB formula—beans, bacon, and bannock. With these three staples for ammunition, the long abused frying pan becomes a threatening weapon indeed. Shaw took one look at what the skillet wielder was dishing out. Then he stepped politely out of line.

"That's a deadly looking mess," he whispered agreeably to an acquaintance in way of explanation.

This bushman repeated the phrase with an appreciative grin, although not so softly. The long chided cook—who, after all, had been doing his best for the company with an economical fare on which many a northerner has thrived satisfactorily enough for years—punctuated his resignation by hurling the nearest frying pan. It hit the chuckling bushman and dislocated his kneecap.

Reginald W. Shaw, who'd handled pots and pans some as has every backwoods bachelor, was hired to man the cook stove. His name from then on, of course, was Deadly. Vagaries of pronunciation modified it over the years to the less startling Dudley.

"Are you sure you've breakfasted?" I asked Dudley when he returned some fifteen minutes later.

"Gouged myself copiously, yes," he rejoindered with a twinkle. "I'm glutted with vast quantities of flippers and tiger."

"Flippers?" I repeated.

"Flapjacks," interpreted Dudley Shaw.

"And. . . .and tiger?" I asked.

"Bacon," the small man translated. "That's because it's striped. Sounds nobler when called tiger."

Our neighbor told me, between draughts rather than sips of tea, how northerners make their bread. Sourdough bread was what I wanted, he said. This mining camp sustenance had early proved its ability to rise in any temperature short of freezing. On very cold nights though, Dudley admitted seriously, he sometimes took the batter to bed with him.

During the gold rush days at the turn of the century, when prospectors stampeded past here toward where Yukon nuggets lay yellow and beckoning beneath the aurora polaris, miners used to bake sourdough bread in the shallow steel vessels they used for panning gold. Some of them still do for that matter, Dudley asserted.

A shallow hole was scooped in the ground, often in the heat-retaining sand of a stream bank. A fire was allowed to burn to coals in this cavity. Dough, in the meantime, was rising between two gold pans. Some of the glowing embers and hot sand was shoved out of the hole. The pans were set in the depression and covered with the hot residue. An hour's cooking in this outdoor oven was generally the minimum. The bread wouldn't burn if allowed to stay longer, but the crust would thicken and become more golden brown.

A simple bush method for starting the sourings necessary for this breadstuff, Dudley said, is to mix four cups of flour with enough warm water to make a thick creamy batter. Two tablespoons of sugar may be added. So may two teaspoons of salt. The mixture should be placed in a warm spot for upwards of two days to sour. Yeastcake dissolved in warm water may be added to hasten the fermentation which will then usually take place over night. Some find it handier to include instead a tablespoon of some cooking acid such as vinegar, also used to revive aged sourings.

"Cover the sourings loosely," Dudley cautioned, "or they'll explode frightfully all over the place. Makes a ghastly mess. Remember they bubble copiously to better than double size, so use a container that's vast enough. A lard pail's our favorite up in these jungles."

The initial loaves are made, Dudley went on, by mixing three-fourths of this sourdough with a tablespoon of melted fat and a cup of flour into which a teaspoon of baking soda has been well stirred. Then add whatever additional flour may be necessary to make a smoothly kneading dough.

"Keep attacking," Dudley cautioned. "Don't gentle it. That's where most women make their mistake. Too much pushing and pressing lets the gas escape that's needed to raise the stuff. Just bang the dough together in a hurry, cut off loaves to fit your pans, and put them in a warm place to raise."

The batch, once it has plumped out to double size, should be baked from forty minutes to an hour in a warm oven that's preferably hottest the first fifteen minutes. If I had an oven thermometer, Dudley recommended with an exactness that surprised me, I could start the bread at 400° and finish it at 375°. I gave Brad a smug look. So I'd have no use for that oven thermometer I'd secretly tucked in a duffle bag, wouldn't I?

Baking should redouble the size of the loaves, Dudley went on, pretending not to notice the exchange of glances. One tested "in the usual way." He elucidated that the usual way was to wait until the loaf seemed crisply browned, then jab in a straw. If the bread was done, the straw would come out dry and clean.

"How about the quarter of the sourdough I don't use?" I inquired, scribbling down the formula.

"That would be your start for future sourdough," Dudley

said, "if it weren't for the fact that I'm going to give you some sourings that are fourteen years old."

"Fourteen years?" I gasped. "Isn't that a lot?"

"They've just started nicely," Dudley beamed proudly. "You can keep them going by dropping in chunks of left over flippers, bread, and such, or just plain flour and water. Always leave out at least a cup to keep going with. When the mixture gets too rampageous, a touch of baking soda will gentle it. Don't use soda too copiously though, or you'll bog down the sourdough for good."

"Dave was saying that if to much soda's used, it makes the bread yellowish," Brad put in. "But if you don't get in enough, then the stuff tastes sour."

"Takes experience. Even when someone tells you how, it still takes experience," Dudley nodded. He looked up suddenly. "How's the enemy?"

"The what?" I said, puzzled.

"The enemy? The time?" Dudley interpreted, eyes blinking amiably behind thick lensed spectacles. "Got to start rambling again before I'm glutted. Really stopped by to tell you about the dance Saturday. It's going to be down in Ted Boynton's notorious old restaurant. Folks hope you can come, especially as it's mostly in your honor. Sort of a blinking get-together dance, that is. One of the cheerful local customs."

"Oh, I hope no one is going to a lot of trouble," I started, but Dudley interrupted with a dry chuckle.

"No trouble," Dudley said, and he chuckled again. "Good excuse."

"I'll need a haircut," Brad mused.

"A safety razor and a comb work gloriously for me. There's only two weeks between a bad haircut and a good haircut, anyway." He reached for his ancient felt hat. "I had to get one the other day myself. When I went to the Bay, Dave mistook me for a pelt. Worst of it is, the blighter graded me as a Number Three, Small."

He sniffed the wind that gusted in when he opened the door.

"Thank you for the tea. Noble lap," he decreed. "Guess I'd better start snowshoeing joyously again before it gets too cold, if I'm going to trap some plunder for the Hudson's Bay Company. Got to stay off jawbone."

"Jawbone?" Brad, this time, repeated in a perplexed voice.

"Debt," translated Dudley. "Ghastly."

CHAPTER ELEVEN

WHAT IS COLD?

"None is so poor that he need sit on a pumpkin," Thoreau had written. "That is shiftlessness."

So while Brad's knee was mending, we concentrated on building furniture for our wilderness home. Snow was still sifting down outside. The pellets were harder now. When gusts of wind whined out of the restless forest, the particles rattled against the cabin like gravel.

Brad built a bunk for me in the northeast corner of the room. A single post was enough to support the two spruce poles that, with the front and side walls, framed a comfortably large rectangle seven feet long by nearly half that width. Boards provided a trim flat surface upon which a partially inflated air mattress bulged softly beneath my 90-by-90 eiderdown sleeping robe.

I could lie with my head near the aromatic logs and gaze out the four banked windows. The view was so enthralling that we would have followed Thoreau's example about curtains if for no other reason.

"It costs me nothing for curtains," Thoreau had observed, "for I have no gazers to shut out but the sun and the moon, and I am willing that they should look in. The moon will not sour milk nor taint meat of mine, nor will the sun injure my furniture or fade my carpet. If he is sometimes too warm a friend, I find it still better economy to retreat behind some curtain which nature has provided than to add a single item to the details of housekeeping."

Most of our other furniture problems were solved as easily, our cabin being so small. To save space, Brad built a trundle bed for himself. During the daytime, it shoved out of the way beneath my bunk. Braces were omitted across the inner side. The result was that, although he sometimes had the unsteady impression of being on shipboard when rolling over during the night, duffle bags could be left stored beneath the permanent bunk which we had decided to make higher than usual for this reason. Enough boards were left over to fashion a handy multitude of shelves.

We already had some furnishings such as the cooking stove, of course, and the air-tight heater and folding table we had brought from Hudson Hope. A substantial kitchen cabinet, with drawers and compartments of light box wood, proved easy to assemble. An orange crate, steadied with a broad top and base, became a typewriter stand for our compact portable. Picturesque corner posts of unpeeled birch provided additional reinforcement for this.

"I had three chairs in my house," said Thoreau, "one for solitude, two for friendship, and three for society."

So did we; by aid of inheritance, one's being on hand when we arrived. This moosehide armchair, which creaked so agreeably as it adapted itself to our weights, was our favorite from the first. We built two smaller chairs for use with table and typewriter stand. Experimentation revealed that the seats should be a foot lower than the tops of these latter. We made the seats somewhat larger than the usual dining room size and pitched them and the backs slightly backward for additional comfort. I sandpapered the pieces after Brad had measured and cut them. Then I gingerly held, while he nailed.

Cold deepened during the day. Thinning flurries of sharp-edged snow rustled over the roof, then ceased entirely. When I went out that dusk to get some eggs from where we kept them frozen in the cache, I noted that the thermometer outside our door registered two degrees below zero. The storehouse is no more than fifty yards away, but by the time I returned the red line of alcohol hovered at seven degrees below zero. The temperature had dropped another fourteen degrees by the time we went to bed.

The colored fluid in the glass gauge was down to fifty degrees below zero the next morning. Haze, like smoke, hung some twenty feet above the frozen ground. Mist clouded upwards from the two black stretches of open water that rent the ice of the Peace River. Northern Lights and a full moon made a ghostly thing of the slow subarctic dawn.

Shrubbery and trees sagged under furry white frost an inch thick. The heavy red sun, when it finally swelled into view, glowered through the blanched wilderness like a ghostly Christmas Tree decoration. Cold billowed inward like fog the moment I pulled open our rime-framed door.

Breath hung suspended in the outside air. I was surprised that the day didn't feel particularly cold. Then the frigidness gripped with astounding speed. The thin upper portion of my right ear froze, as I was hurrying toward the woodpile. It thawed as quickly, evidently because of the pressure induced by my exertion. There was a startling pop. Before I realized what was going on, the same thing happened in the upper arc of the other ear.

"Here, let me give you a hand with that wood," Brad said, surprisingly nearby.

"I'll do this. You take care of your leg."

"My leg's okay." He did a cautious jig in the snow to bolster the statement. "Say, isn't this terrific! I've always wondered what real cold would be like."

The unexpectedness of seeing his eyebrows wreathed with

hoar made me laugh. I expected more of a reaction when I told him about it, but he just grinned and continued heaping his crooked left arm high with split poplar.

When we stamped back into the cabin, he led me to a mirror. My eyebrows were blanched, too. The moisture in my breath had also left the hair closest to my face fuzzy with whiteness. The frost quickly melted in the heat of the room, leaving our complexions glowing and exhilarated. My ears were red and the least bit tender, but they never bothered further.

Smoke plumed straight upward from the cabin's stovepipe that day, a pillar that seemed to be supporting an iridescent ceiling of mist above the throbbing earth. There was not the minutest suggestion of wind. Yet there was none of the "eternal Northern silence" that some who evidently stay warmly south describe with such vividness. Trees cannonaded, their innermost structures torn by freezing and expanding sap. River ice snarled and boomed. When coyotes yipped momentarily up near the mouth of Box Canyon, they seemed grey and skulking. The huge dark body of a moose crashed through the now pallid willows by the brook which, its protesting channels clotting, overflowed and froze anew in a slowly broadening pattern.

"What are Dudley Shaw and the other trappers doing today," I wondered from the luxuriousness of the big armchair over which I'd warmly draped my eiderdown.

"Sitting it out," Brad supposed, looking up from Dumas's *Vicomte De Bragelonne*. "Fur doesn't move any more than necessary in weather like this, anyway. But what a day to lounge by the stove with a good book!"

"It's downright cozy," I agreed, turning a page of Emerson's *Essays*.

It was extraordinarily cozy. This feeling was heightened by the undercurrent of excitement. Far from the humdrum concerns of man-made civilization, we appreciated as never

before the simple necessities of life. . . . shelter, food, clothing, and warmth. The cold intensified.

When I awoke that night, I remembered Brad's saying
how Edward R. Frude had told his science class that there
is no such thing as cold. Frude had been athletic director as
well as science teacher at Kimball Union Academy, and he
made it as plain as he could that what is called "cold" is
merely the absence of heat, just as black and white are not
really colors but the lack of color.

The chill that penetrated to my bones as I crawled reluctantly from the eiderdown seemed an active substance, however, a congealing liquid that had seeped into every cranny
of the ashen wilderness. The overnight fire in the heater had
subsided to a feeble murmur that, momentarily boisterous
when I opened the lid to add wood, chortled briefly about
the cabin before shadows chased its drowsy flicker back into
the iron stronghold.

What I saw, though, when I glanced out a frost-clear
patch of window made me forget I was shivering.

"Brad," I guess I almost whispered.

The Aurora Borealis was abroad in the wintry sky. It put
me in mind of the glowing body of a tremendous dinosaur,
wondrous rather than terrifying, cavorting on a radiant
swamp whose shores were the electric blue of night. Shallow
waves moved ceaselessly, their planes opalescent with mingling shades. Eddies, cross currents, and broadening pools
swirled and quivered with magic tints among which the silvery green of chatoyant nephrite jade was dominant.

The spectacle, which seemed at cumulus cloud height although it was from 60 to 400 miles above the frozen earth,
engulfed more and more of the sky. Charged particles from
the now hidden sun—attracted toward the poles of the
earth's magnetic field in characteristic bands, arc, curtains,
beams, and coronas—were exciting the atoms and molecules
of gas in the upper atmosphere and causing them to emit

light. It seemed almost as if the sherbet chips of stars were melting one by one, and were licked up by the scintillating reptile.

"Not even Thoreau ever saw the likes of that," blended a voice with my thoughts, and I realized that Brad had been warm beside me for indistinguishable moments. "I remember watching it once in prep school, one twenty-below-zero night in New Hampshire. A big fellow named Ralph Smith, who could tear them apart on the football field, got down on his knees. He thought the world was coming to an end."

"It makes headlines around Boston," I noted, "and it's never one-millionth like this. It's. . . . it's sort as if we're standing behind the scenes, where human beings aren't usually admitted."

Sixty-three degrees below zero! Nearly one hundred degrees below freezing! That's how cold it became outside our cabin the next day—the coldest we've ever experienced in northern British Columbia. Such a frigid spell, we would like to emphasize, is unusual. Fear of winters shouldn't keep anyone away from the North.

Less snow falls in many parts of Alaska and northern Canada than in such an American city as Chicago. Horses in the vicinity of Hudson Hope maintain themselves by grazing the year around. Temperatures, even in the frosty interior of the northwestern continental corner, drop little if any lower than in Montana and North Dakota.

Blizzards are entirely unknown where we live. Extreme cold, when it does arrive, is dramatic. Such periods are often followed by summery chinook winds which the Indians call *snow-eaters*. There are generally only a few really severe days during any of our winters. The ground is often still bare and the temperature mild on Christmas. The weather was dramatic now. I wouldn't have missed the experience for anything.

What is cold? It's when rubber becomes brittle. It's when

the graphite in a so-called lead pencil becomes so hard it will only make a colorless groove on paper. It's when metal becomes as granular as a stick of peppermint candy, when axes if not warmed beforehand can shiver to fragments at a stroke, and when a saw blade shatters instead of bending. It's when touching a steel stirrup with the bare hand is like fingering a red-hot horseshoe. The flesh is actually seared.

Cold is when paraffin melts so slowly that a candle will scarcely burn. Cold is when coal oil solidifies, and the flame will sputter out on the wick. Cold is when gas lines clog with ice even when Alaska Highway trucks are roaring along at top power. Cold is when some popular anti freezes become blocks of ice in their unopened containers. Cold is when your flashlight dies out in your hand.

Cold is when ink has to be diluted with glycerine. It's long after mercury freezes. Quicksilver becomes rigid at a mere thirty-eight degrees below zero, while grain alcohol will remain liquid at minus 179°. Cold is when a sourdough can tell how potent his liquor is by the amount of ice crystals rattling inside the bottle.

"Here's our chance to find out if saliva will freeze before it reaches the ground," Brad laughed. It won't, he concluded, Jack London and a lot of other writers who should have known better to the contrary.

When the water we bailed from the newly chopped opening in the brook spattered on previously frozen spatterings, however, these crackled and snapped like firecrackers. Similar phenomena may have given support to the saliva legend. Even when we took turns with the ax, that slight exertion made our lungs burn. We each filled a bucket and hurried back toward the sanctuary of the cabin.

"Listen," I said, pausing spellbound.

Our breaths, freezing as they left our mouths, swished about us like silk. The millions of tiny ice particles shimmered gently before our eyes with every color of a ghostly spectrum.

When the contents of Brad's bucket slopped over as he banged the door behind us, the water became a hard white curl on the floor before I could mop it up. It seemed almost impossible to heat the single log room, although we piled in fuel until the air-tight heater was cherry red. Unseasoned wood had been transformed into icy chunks that retarded the fire for long minutes. When Brad tried to split some green birch, the ax bounced ineffectually until some particular blow would cause the block to snap apart. Even the well aged cabin logs shrunk, letting in more cold. Every visible nail was dotted with frost. Butter hardened between stove and bannock.

Everything, after three days of such low temperatures, seemed unnatural. Uneasy, we couldn't sit still. Some unfathomable tension gripped sky, ground, and spirit.

"Will it ever be warm again?" I almost despaired.

That afternoon we saw the sun apparently burst and cascade earthward in a molten confusion of fiery drops as whirling ice crystals stole its iridescence. A beam seemed to shoot like a heavenly arrow through the remains of the golden heart. This baffling spectral ray quivered inexorably parallel to the bleached horizon.

Then as if two hoops from the sun's rim were rolling into balance, a strange new celestial body shone into being at each end of the shaft. Hollow, these mock suns glowed with scarlets and crimsons and seething greenish yellows. Never had I ever seen anything more exquisite. I could hardly breathe.

"Sun dogs," I heard Brad saying. "The weather is going to break."

I thought of all that when several weeks later I received a newspaper clipping enclosed in a letter. "Cold Wave Grips Boston," the headline read. "Fifteen Above by Night."

The frosty fireworks of the Aurora Polaris had again recaptured the great rarefied shell of the ionosphere by the time we blew out the coal oil lamp that evening. The red column of alcohol in the thermometer outside still hovered more than ninety degrees below freezing.

Yet what awakened me early the next morning, sweltering in my eiderdown, was the noise of dripping water. I twisted uneasily in my hot sleeping robe. The sound persisted, and I thought I caught the gentle murmur of wind.

"Hear that?" a voice chuckled, and I saw Brad hunched up on one elbow, regarding me.

"It sounds like water dripping from the roof."

"That's right," he agreed unexpectedly. "The snow is melting."

"How can the snow be melting?" I started to jump to the floor. "The cabin isn't on fire?"

"No, no, everything's all right," he said with hurried reassurance. "It's chinooking."

CHAPTER TWELVE

CHINOOK

"I should not obtrude my affairs so much on the notice of my readers," Thoreau said early in his account, "if very particular inquiries had not been made concerning my mode of life."

The words had been penned a century before, but they seemed as ageless as the wilderness river along whose icy floor we were moving toward Hudson Hope. Hadn't Brad and I been beset with similar questions even before I had tucked the first carefully selected indispensables into the canvas duffle bags that are the trunks of the farther places?

Wouldn't we feel terribly alone among strangers, city acquaintances asked? How could I help but be terrified when left by myself in our cabin? Why had we decided to settle in such a remote place? How many Christmases would we be away—this from a young boy, Jack Otis. Suppose an Indian should happen upon me while I was swimming, presumedly unclothed, in some woodland stream—this from a Back Bay spinster who when the colored comic sections arrived with the Sunday papers laid them resolutely aside, not to be enjoyed until Monday.

"I should not talk so much about myself if there was anybody whom I knew as well," Thoreau apologized before an-

87

swering such queries. "Unfortunately, I am confined to this theme by the narrowness of my experience."

That is also our excuse.

Our answer to the first and the most predominant question, asked us in innumerable forms, is that we've never met folks so whole-heartedly friendly as those in the North. In such cities as Boston and New York, and no doubt in many another about which we don't happen to know personally, one can dwell in the same apartment house for years and have no more than a nodding acquaintance with a handful of neighbors. But here, after less than a month on the Peace River, we were going to the log settlement because Dudley Shaw had told us that a get-acquainted dance had been arranged for that evening.

As for the other inquiries just enumerated, I'd felt a lot more secure so far when alone than I had on many city occasions. We'd come such a distance because we wanted to settle in pleasant, primitive wilderness where there would be opportunity to live off the country. We hoped to be able to make our home here as long as we wanted. And it had been too cold so far for swimming.

How were we now traveling through this wintry realm as yet little vexed by man? Were we wearing the rugged snowshoes of the local Cree and Beaver Indians, manufactured back in New Brunswick and sold them through the Hudson's Bay Company? No, then probably we were skiing on the long birch runners fashioned by hand here according to Scandinavian precedent by Charlie Ohland and Gunnar Johnson? Not that, either? Oh, of course, we must be riding behind the yelping, panting race of a dog team?

"They'll never believe us when I write them about it," I laughed, swerving around a hummock.

"Who could blame them?" Brad grunted, leaping a crack. "I wouldn't myself. Do you remember how I carefully ex-

plained we weren't going to a winter resort when you first
suggested bringing those skates along?"

"That," I admitted, "is why I had to tie each pair secretly
inside that green tarpaulin and then roll the whole bundle in
my own eiderdown. Now aren't you glad?"

"Women," he decreed solemnly, "never cease to be amazing."

One does not ordinarily skate along a wilderness river in
the subarctic. Pressure, snow, breakups, and always varying
water levels generally combine to leave the icy surface of a
northern stream a rough and jumbled mass.

The three days we'd just had of extreme cold, however,
had clogged the regular channel with ice. The waters of the
Peace River are always flowing on their extreme journey of
more than 2500 miles, even when the great stream is somno-
lent with winter, so now these waters overflowed. This excess
of moisture, filling crevices and depressions as it swelled upward and outward, had solidified so quickly that it remained
a glassy bulge along either shore. Down this we glided, holding out our arms to catch the impetus of the chinook wind
that warmed our backs.

"Look at how this river slants downhill," Brad noted,
skirting a pool of sparkling water. "I'm just as glad we'll be
riding back with Ted Boynton and a load of groceries."

"I hope they don't cost too much," I sighed. "The nestegg's
getting low."

The trough of the wide river channel, bounded by the
shore itself and then by yellowish cutbanks and eventually
by wooded hills, was suffused with intense blue that filled it
like liquid dye. Above this profundity, the hues lost satura-
tion and gained in brilliance as they varied through powder
blues, lilacs, and mauves until finally shading into pinks.

High clouds, bright with the still hidden sun, were serene
yellows and golds against a pale azure sky too remote to

be influenced by the earthbound river. Lower wind-hurtled
clouds, streaming from the purple west toward the carnation-
pink horizon in the east, took on the chromatic tints characteristic to their elevations.

Few spectacles during a northern winter, I decided, can
be lovelier than the gentle coloration of a chinook. The ice
and snow of the river were relieved by the blue-deepened
reflections caught by pools and streaks of overflow. There
was the occasional roar of green water, rushing from beneath
the enslaving ice to have a burst of freedom before being
imprisoned again. Snow-garlanded banks were festooned a
half mile below the cabin with huge icicles, the frozen output
of springs.

The loose bark of birch trees fluttered gayly. Emerald conifers and pearl grey poplars swayed before the west wind
whose warmth was intermingled with pockets of caught-up
cold. It was like standing just inside a big city department
store on a winter day and feeling a sudden bitter draft whenever someone bustled in from the street.

"Isn't this some country?" Brad marveled.

Chinooks here start as warm damp winds from an arm of
the Pacific Ocean, so warmed by the Japanese Current that
the winters in Alaskan seacoast towns west of us are not as
extreme as those in cherry-blossoming Washington, D. C.
The heavy winds lose their moisture in the mountains. By
the time they reach here, they're as balmy as a spring breeze.

Several Canada geese honked at us from the small islands
opposite Dudley's cabin. They came early to these ice-bound
sanctuaries, Dudley said. Geese had been nesting there for
years. Alexander Mackenzie had noted their presence when
lining upriver in 1793 on his way west of the Rockies and
the Coast Range.

Fresh game trails were everywhere. The wilderness had
come alive again under the velvet insistence of the dry west-
erly. The temperature had been 40° Fahrenheit when we'd

left the cabin, a rise of more than one hundred degrees in less than twelve hours. By the time we reached Hudson Hope, the heat along the dazzling river had reached a sweltering 87° in the sun.

The dance was held in Ted Boynton's old restaurant, a log building where short-order meals had been served when mining activity in Hudson Hope was greater. Analyses show that the bright clean coal here, with a heat value of up to more than 15,000 British Thermal Units per pound and an ash content ranging to less than two per cent, is among the best in the world. But markets are far away, and the only present way to get the fuel out is to truck it over a dirt road which is often impassable.

Several of Ted's old signs still decorated the hewn wall: "Don't make fun of our coffee. You'll be old and weak yourself someday."—and—"Use less sugar and stir like hell. We don't mind the noise."

One trapper came in seventy miles on snowshoes for that dance. It's still difficult for me to understand how *moccasin telegraph*—information exchanged by word of mouth and by personally delivered messages—can spread news so rapidly through a nearly deserted wilderness.

If I'd been expecting something between a Virginia Reel and an Indian war dance, I would have been greatly mistakened. It was the same as any small good-humored dance in many rural American communities, if those we've attended have been any criterion, except that folks because of their potential dependency upon one another on account of the remoteness of the region seem even friendlier. They didn't bother with waiting around for introductions. Instead, they asked us if we'd like a sandwich, or a drink, and did we feel like taking a turn around the floor? Women took turns in selecting partners, too. Brad liked it when Clara Barkley and Jessie Murphy invited him, although it surprised him when they thanked him afterwards.

"I told them it should be I who was doing the thanking," he explained to me. "They and these other gals can really dance."

Most of the folks were usually graceful and light footed which was only natural, I decided, for people living a healthy outdoor life. There were fox trots, waltzes, and a lot of fast polkas. There was more noise than one might have expected from a group of less than three dozen. It was all exuberant and good humored, though, and it helped to keep gaiety at a high pitch.

When anyone felt like laughing, he laughed right out. If he had something to say, it was something he'd just as soon remark in at least conversational tones. Feet stamped. Voices raised. There was a lot of drinking straight from bottles, politely in the darkness of the kitchen, but the effects were immediately expanded in boisterous hearty fun. Marvalee Murphy and Ruth Blair took turns in making a small accordion echo like an orchestra.

We didn't meet many people that night as far as actual numbers went. We did meet a large percentage of Hudson Hope's population, however, before and during the affair. A surprising number of them became intimate friends. That's saying a lot, particularly here in the wilderness. Being a friend up here in the farther places really means something.

Suppose you're a trapper and weeks after your accustomed time for coming out with your winter's catch you still haven't appeared? So some other bushman hoists a pack on his back and starts walking to your main cabin. Suppose some destitute old timer falls ill, and the men who happen to know about it not only chip in the money necessary for immediate hospital care, but they rush him personally to Fort St. John by whatever means is possible, no matter what the weather?

Plain ordinary acquaintants, even avowed enemies who

haven't spoken to one another for years, will do that much as a matter of course. Being a friend means a great deal more. Here, surrounded by elemental nature, is where one appreciates and needs amity. Here one, hearing of a friend in trouble, doesn't ask, "What can I do to help?" One just wants to know, "Where is he?"

Everyone had such a good time at the dance that no one wanted to leave. The women had brought plenty of sandwiches. Dave and Marion Cuthill had fetched olives, pickles, and other dainties from the Hudson's Bay Company. Ted and Ivy Boynton kept coffee steaming on the stove.

It was nearly five o'clock in the morning before Brad and I started to go next door to the hotel, and then Dave and Marion wouldn't hear of it. They insisted that we take the spare bedroom in the Hudson's Bay Company house. It didn't require much persuading. Both of us had liked them instantly. Besides, I'd just been itching to see what sort of living quarters the Governor and Company of Adventurers of England trading into Hudson's Bay furnished its representatives.

"The twin beds are all made up," Marion was insisting.

"We can all have breakfast together whenever we feel like getting up," Dave put in, "and then I'll get together that grubstake you want."

"Well," Brad hesitated, looking at me.

"We'd love to," I decided.

CHAPTER THIRTEEN

HUDSON'S BAY COMPANY

If you've been to many movies, you will probably be able as we were to picture the Hudson's Bay Company house as a massive log structure. You'll realize that the builders inserted only a few small windows so as to conserve the heat from great open fireplaces into which whole logs are fed. Perhaps you, too, will be able almost to feel the yielding shag of wolf and grizzly pelts that soften the whipsawed floor.

Near-record heads of mountain sheep and goat give a cozy effect to the walls, some may agree, especially when the lights from brightly scoured kerosene lamps glint from the curving horns. What would be the most comfortable chair in such a Post but a picturesque ingenuity of deerskin, stretched loosely over a gigantic spread of moose antlers? As for the actual trading store, could it be more appropriately separated from the rustic living quarters than by a massive slab door across which a hewn oaken bar is ceremoniously dropped after business hours?

That is the way the homes of Hudson's Bay Company fur traders, generally referred to along Vine Street as factors, do look in many motion pictures.

The Cuthill's house, which would never make the grade at

most Hollywood studios, was a trim two-story modernity of plywood. Neat white walls and a traditional red roof concealed the compact insulation that guarded against temperature extremes. The numerous cheerful windows were double glazed. Instead of one pane of glass, that is, there were always two with an insulative inert-air space between.

There was a cellar and a furnace. Dave called the latter a circulator hot-air heater. It operated on coal from King Gething's mine on Bullhead Mountain above town. Dave explained its almost automatic functions with fond minuteness. The cellar also flourished a gasoline generator that periodically charged a bank of modern storage batteries. Besides electric lights, the dwelling also boasted the latest style of washing machine.

The bungalow had been furnished by the Company with no less than 2700 different items, as a matter of fact. A comprehensive library, largely of books about the northern life in which the Cuthills were particularly interested, was freely supplemented with additional volumes each year.

Fur rugs? There had been a small wolverine skin between the guest room's twin beds with their innerspring mattresses. But it had shed hair that eventually got on the tundra-brown upholstery of the living room suite, Marion said, and on the Axminsters.

The bathroom was a trim arrangement of sparkling efficiency. So was the gay kitchen with its innumerable gadgets that caught my eye. All in all, our rather expensive apartment in the choice Back Bay section of Boston had not been nearly as attractive and modern. The only utility we'd had that Marion lacked was an electric refrigerator. She was having to get along, for the time being, on an icebox for which Bill Carter cut great cold blocks every winter and stowed them under sawdust in the nearby icehouse.

"Thank goodness," admitted Marion who'd been a nurse

in Saskatchewan before marrying Dave, then a HB.C. apprentice just landed from Scotland. "Otherwise, I'd probably find myself not appreciating all these other things."

Ted Boynton had promised at the dance to bring his sleigh around in front of the Bay about noon to haul our supplies upriver. The trip would cost another five dollars, although most reasonably so, I thought. Our nestegg was dwindling quickly.

Once abed, I lay and stared about me for a long time. This Hudson's Bay Company house in which we were staying could not have cost less than $12,000. All this had to be paid for out of profits, I thought dully. What would our groceries cost? I gave a deep sigh. It must have been louder than I thought, for Brad stirred.

"Anything the matter?" he asked drowsily. "Didn't you have a good time?"

"A wonderful time," I breathed. "All this has been wonderful. Oh, I don't ever want to leave it."

"Why should we leave it?" he asked sleepily, missing the point, and a few moments later was breathing deeply and regularly.

Late the next morning, after Fort Garry coffee and hot cakes crisscrossed with sizzling Canada bacon, we thanked Dave and Marion. They saw us to the door. Then Dave, clapping on an otter skin cap, transformed from host to storekeeper. No longer were we guests, although the difference in atmosphere was so slight that I wondered if I weren't imagining things. But it was as customers that we went with him along the high board walk toward the modern trading store.

"Have a look around," Dave invited, as we followed him through the back entrance. "Watch out for that open trap door. . . . I've got to go down there and start the fire. It'll just take a moment."

Circumventing the dark rectangle where steps led to a

The heating plant.

The pantry deluxe.

shadowy cellar, I followed Brad past the small office on the right with its northern maps and its small black safe. Some tools and shavings were scattered about, as if someone had been doing some carpentry there. When we came to the shelf-lined, country-bisected store I just stood still and took in deep breaths.

"Uummm," I enthused so avidly that Brad gave me an apprehensive glance.

Then he sniffed, grinned, and inhaled appreciatively, although I realized that odors weren't as important to him as they are to me. I tell myself that perhaps it's because he had his nose smashed playing football, but I realize there's probably a natural difference, too. Sensitivities vary with individuals, and my sense of smell has always been a little more important than most of my other perceptions.

You've never smelled anything really exciting, I thought, until you've lingered inside a Hudson's Bay Company fur trading post. The arousal I'd felt when visiting Molinard's world-famous perfumery at Grasse, on the Riviera, seemed effete by comparison. The odor of moosehide moccasins, tanned by the Indians over smoky fires, was assailing my nostrils deliciously. The scent of traps, venerable Point Blankets whose markings once indicated their price in terms of beaver skins, and raw pelts mingled with the thrilling metallic pungency of double-bitted axes and well oiled rifles. Gently insistent was the soul-stirring aroma of the fur press where, winters and springs, thousands of dollars in furs were baled and sealed for shipment Outside.

There was a can-rattling bang beneath me, and then a steady low-throated roar sent dress-stirring air up through the grill at my feet. We later learned that a favorite although not favored way of quickly starting a coal fire in the North is by standing back and pitching lighted matches into a cold bed of fuel over which gasoline has been freshly poured. The trouble is that enough unsuspected heat may remain among

the old ashes to vaporize the petrol at an even more dangerous speed than is ordinary. Then a roof-lifting blast can and
sometimes does result.

The burr of a voice, imprecating some unmentionable
wood-butchering carpenter for having been such a defiled
fool as to lay an unchaste fire that profane way, indicated
that Dave must be back upstairs. He appeared, a streak of
black on one cheek and his fur headpiece at a new angle.

I turned just as he heaved a slab of bacon casually on the
scales. He allowed as how it'd come to $3.50 even. My fore-
head wrinkled with mental arithmetic. Then I recollected
that United States dollars were worth $1.10 in Canadian
money at the moment and started again. Why, the bacon
we'd been buying from Mr. Rogers on Newbury Street, and
from John's in the opposite block, had cost more than that.

I started to relax. Just then Dave Cuthill admitted that a
tin of powdered eggs actually sold for $2.20. Brad seeing my
horrified glance, hastily injected that four dozen dehydrated
eggs didn't take up much space, did they?

My smile was just returning when I noticed that a tin of
pumpkin powder that Brad had set to one side wore a $3.70
label. It was the Post manager who marveled at 100 pounds
of choice fresh pumpkin being concentrated into 1-25th
that weight. I gave up at this and started to wander around
the store once more.

Cheese, butter, and other staples were no more expensive
than they had been Outside. Canned goods, on the other
hand, ran as much as fifty per cent higher because of transportation charges. But instead of canned peaches, for instance, there were fat and much more practical dried
peaches. We were going to make out for awhile longer, anyway.

I hesitated at a pile of bright shallow vessels resembling
broad, low dishpans. I'd seen others like them rusting behind
the deserted cabins upriver.

"Gold-pans," Dave Cuthill identified unexpectedly.

I looked from the sleek brown fur of the Scotsman's otter cap to his closely shaven ruddy cheeks and neat business atire, complete even to a plaid necktie. Brad had vowed that one reason he was anxious to take to the woods was so that he wouldn't have to wear any more of those choking sense-less vanities of the world of style. Except for the headgear, I thought irrelevantly, Hollywood would have turned thumbs down on David Moody Cuthill as well as his Post.

"Goodness," I heard myself saying, "can you sell gold pans for a dollar?"

Mr. Cuthill looked at Brad and then back at me, and he cleared his throat.

"I mean," Dave Cuthill said carefully, "you fill one of these pressed-steel pans with gravel and water. You swirl the mix-ture, dipping the pan in the stream occasionally to wash out the lighter dirt and such that's in suspension. You end up with the gold if any. Gold, being heavy, naturally works to the bottom."

"Oh," I said. It took a moment to sink in. Then I exclaimed, "Could I do it?"

"Why now," Dave Cuthill allowed conservatively, "there's color in most of the gravel bars along the upper river here. If you didn't get discouraged, you might pan enough after the ice goes out to make some mighty special jewelry for yourself. There's always the chance, too, that you might hit a rich pocket."

I reached for the topmost pan.

"We'll take one," I said decisively.

CHAPTER FOURTEEN

AREN'T YOU LONELY?

The question most often asked us is, "Aren't you lonely?"
Thoreau, too, was belabored with similar queries. His response was that he'd never found the companion that was so
companionable as solitude.

We are for the most part more lonely when we go aboard
among men, he pointed, than when we stay in our rooms.
I'd learned the truth of that long before going to the woods.
The lonesomest I've felt was when walking up New York's
crowded Fifth Avenue, alone and a stranger, one Spring
afternoon.

"Men frequently say to me," recounted Thoreau, "I should
think you would feel lonesome down there and want to be
nearer to folks, rainy and snowy days and nights especially.
I am tempted to reply to such, what sort of space is that
which separates a man from his fellows and makes him solitary? I have found that no exertion of the legs can bring two
minds much nearer to one another."

There can be no very black melancholy to him who lives
in the midst of nature and still has his senses, Thoreau decided. Even if we had never proved any other part of his
philosophy to ourselves, we would soon have confirmed that,

for it must be even more true today than it could have been during the comparatively unrestrained yesterdays.

"I am no more lonely than the loon in the pond that laughs so loud," compared Thoreau. "I am no more lonely than a single dandelion in a pasture, or a bean leaf, or sorrel, or a horsefly. I am no more lonely than the brook, or a weather-cock, or the north star, or an April shower, or a January thaw, or the first spider in a new house."

Neither are Brad and I. The closest we ever come to it, I guess, is when we're seized with the wish that Rita and Tom Gray, or Mildred and David Prince, or Beth and Charlie Brent could be here to share some particularly delightful experience with us.

City friends had been adamant in their warnings of the privations we would have to endure. But when we sat down to baked beaver tail and beans—and when we passed care-free days reveling in Dumas, Farnol, Stevenson, and other entertaining writers for whom we'd never been able to spare the time in "civilization"—we wondered just how much hardship there was to this new life.

Brad had been yearning more or less hopelessly for beaver tail ever since one boyhood day when he'd read among Horace Kephart's long popular outdoor admonitions: "This tidbit of old-time trappers will be tasted by few of our generation, more's the pity."

So when Dan Macdonald left no less than a dozen for us at the Hudson's Bay Company, they were a particular treat. Dangling from a cord, they looked all the world like scaly black fish that had been decapitated and strung by their caudal fins. In fact, I couldn't believe at first that they were anything else.

The lean black haired trapper, so husky that he had once shouldered his pack across the entire fourteen miles of portage from Hudson Hope to the head of Rocky Mountain

Canyon without noticing that Bill Carter had slyly inserted a boulder, had certainly not been hindered by the weight of these delicacies. But we couldn't have been as pleased if he'd brought us a giant flitch of home-smoked bacon, instead. It seemed almost impossible to thank him enough. When he handed us an unexpected paper-wrapped bundle, too, I just couldn't find any more words.

"Beaver quarter," Dan explained, stubby white teeth gleaming. "I was going to fetch one in for Dave, anyway, and he told me you folks was interested in trying different wild foods. No, there's no need to thank me. It was just as easy to fetch two."

Brad added the beaver meat exuberantly to his packsack which already contained a few letters, magazines, books, and a can of Fort Garry baking powder. It was no wonder we didn't feel lonely, walking out of Hudson Hope that mail day.

Anticipation lengthened our strides, rather, as we walked towards the cabin that dusk in the murmurous warmth of a chinook wind that had been blowing for nearly three weeks. It was near the end of March, and the days were sensibly longer. We could hear the hollow ring of Dudley's ax from his woodlot a quarter-mile inland when we passed his cabin on our way to the river. By following the frozen surface, we could cut in half the time and effort needed for the second part of our homeward journey. We stopped only long enough to leave four of the beaver tails with a note and to pick up the long dry poles without which we no longer ventured on the ice.

Then we headed across the end of the wooded island in front of Dudley's toward the cliffs over which our brook toppled. The river channel was suffused with the deep intense color we had come to identify to ourselves as chinook blue. Clouds streaming along the horizon were soft vermilion.

"Well, I'll be doggoned," I heard Brad mutter. "Look at

our tracks. We aren't going to be able to travel this way many more times."

Our clearly outlined footprints of that morning floated ahead of us in several inches of now hardening slush.

I found my first pussy willows of the year a few yards from where we left the river to climb to the flat above. They looked like puffy snowflakes clinging to magic red wands. Together, we gathered a nostalgic armful. Their softness left me alert to hear the chance note of some arriving bird, or a hibernating chipmunk's first chirp, or the footfall of a bear as it ventured out of its winter quarters.

When Brad pulled the latch string and stood aside, I almost hated to go indoors. It was because the approaching springtime smelled so nice. But, I realized as more prosaic things closed about us, the aromatic walls of this new home of ours smelled like a part of the fragrant outdoors, too.

"Tomorrow," Brad sighed expectantly, "we taste the tidbit of old-time trappers."

"Do we scale them like bass?" I wondered.

"Oh, it's a lot easier than that," he promised, with as much aplomb as if he'd been a crony of Kit Carson and the other mountain men of Taos.

Loosened by the surprisingly simple method of propping the tails near an outdoor fire, the rough black hide puffed and could be peeled off in big flakes. The appendages proved so oily that when we left them untended for a few moments, we returned to find one flaming like a torch. The result, if extravagant, was what Brad certified to be, "Delicious nutritious—a gastronomical delight!" Ordinarily, however, we preferred to bake the white pork-like meat all day with beans.

We managed to forego until the third day the beaver quarter which had been carefully skinned, Dan explained, so as not to break any oil sacs. It was so marbled with fat that when I surrounded it with potatoes and onions and set it roasting, no basting was necessary. The odiferous crackling and sputtering kept Brad moving from typewriter to oven door.

"We don't want to overcook it," he excused himself when I caught him spearing a morsel with a hunting knife. "You know we both like our meat rare."

This, fortunately, was true. Most wild meat, except such naturally fat animals as beaver and bear, is so dry that cooking it more than one would a tender portion of lamb ruins it in our estimation. When eleven o'clock came around, we just couldn't wait the additional hour. Up went the wings of the table. Out came the sizzling feast to sit, enthroned before us, on the protective coaster Brad had sawed from the end of a birch log. Nor was the amisk, as the local Crees call it, disappointing.

"Uummm," Brad enthused, "it tastes like particularly succulent goose, doesn't it?"

Our beaver had come from the most desirable of all habitats, a poplar pond, Dudley assured us when he stopped by for lunch the next day.

"Noble creatures," he decreed, anchoring a slab between two slices of the bread he'd brought as his share of the meal. "Glutted himself joyously with poplar."

"How can you tell?" I asked.

"Amisks who bog themselves down on willow," Dudley Shaw explained, "are permeated with a bitterish flavor. And if they're crowded back into spruce, as happens on some congested ponds, the result is notoriously ghastly."

I shuddered feelingly with him as I reached for the teapot.

"Then there's but one thing to do," Dudley went on. "Thanks, that's noble lap. The only thing you can do is parboil it copiously. Indians still scrape fat for a quick snack from even those hides, though. They roast the blinking stuff on green sticks propped by a fire while finishing skinning out the plunder. Cheers them up nobly."

After the meal, we just sprawled around and talked until finally, examining his big watch to see how "the enemy" was coming along, Dudley reckoned he'd better "stagger cheerfully home." First, though, he extracted a carefully sealed bottle from a pocket.

"Here's that sourdough I promised you," he explained, adding proudly, "Fourteen years old. Noble stuff!"

We watched him disappear along the river trail. We were sorry to see him depart but no thoughts of loneliness assailed us. Instead, we at once began an animated conversation about our future.

The banquet had set us wondering anew about the phrase, "Living off the country." Moose, deer, and other such game animals were out of season. Those we saw were so gaunt, anyway, that they would have been poor eating. Perhaps bear, which would be out of hibernation soon, would provide a feasible as well as legal answer. With our funds so low, we were going to need at least a temporary solution.

Brad refused to fret.

"It won't do any good to worry," he stated with a philosophic calmness that seemed almost out of character after his tense city outlook. "Besides, maybe we can get some ideas out of this new batch of books we picked up yesterday."

The Public Library of British Columbia, about which we'd learned from Dudley and the Gethings, had on the basis of a simple application blank started mailing us all the books we could possibly enjoy. We specified volumes from large catalogs on a multitude of subjects they kindly sent us from Victoria. Books had begun arriving almost immediately in nearly every post. There were no fees of any sort. Even postage was paid both ways.

"If we ever strike it rich," Brad averred that afternoon from behind the pages of Hornaday's *Campfires in the Canadian Rockies*, "I don't know of any more deserving outfit than that library to which to bequeath a sizable chunk. Look at this, will you? It tells how to preserve game meat."

Reading is a very important part of log cabin living. Hadn't Thoreau particularly noted, "My residence was more favorable not only to thought, but to reading, than a university?" Publications are not casually allowed to become old here, for the wilderness is a place which has not mislaid time. Local bushmen continue far more soundly in touch with current affairs, as I can testify, than the average subway chaser. Interpretations of cosmopolitan problems are not only followed by radio and recent newspaper. They are painstakingly studied in periodicals handed from one inhabitant to another, often a year or two after the prophecies have or have not come to pass. Some highly paid commentators don't rate pennies along the Peace River.

Finances, not any pangs of loneliness, were our problem. Our money was gone except for less than four dollars we meant to keep for postage. Our cabin was built. Our temporary cache contained enough food to nourish us well into the spring.

"We've really got to start writing," Brad admitted with a look around him. "I sort of hate to tie ourselves down to it, don't you?"

"Let's really pour it on for awhile," I suggested. "The quicker we get set, the sooner we'll be able to make writing a hobby instead of a profession."

The thought aroused so many pleasant visions that except for chores, which mainly had to do with fire and food, we began devoting every workaday hour to plot, theme, atmosphere, and characterization. We were through breakfast and ready to start work as soon as the morning was light enough. We often continued until the sun had set. Except for rare occasions, though, we shunned writing by lamplight. The wilderness was so alive at twilight that working then would have seemed too much like drudgery.

Sometimes at dusk we made our way up Bull Creek which was now a broad highway, inviting us up into the canyons where our water supply had its source in springs that burst from the foot of Bullhead Mountain. Other late afternoons we explored the river and its icy bypaths.

When we had arrived in the North, the sun had not risen above the ridge south of the cabin until after ten o'clock. It had set six hours later.

Now, near the end of March, its incandescent rim arched in sight before nine o'clock. That meant at this latitude that Brad could work outdoors on the wood pile at six o'clock in clear weather and that I could go about cabin chores without a lamp at seven o'clock. There was the same wide hiatus on clear evenings, when the sun disappeared shortly after seven P.M. The lengthening days gave us more and more daylight hours, few of which we could bear to waste. Many evenings we cooked our suppers over outdoor fires built cheerfully high.

Mails came and left but once a week. To save what time we could, we decided to send our stories to a literary agent Brad had once met in New York; one who had no so-called reading fees but who made his living from the ten per cent commission derived from actual sales. We waited breathlessly. It would take at least a month, we figured, before we could fruitfully hope for a response.

Anyway, we assured ourselves, these stories drew a true picture of the North we were beginning to know. The characters weren't eternally lost in blizzards, chased by starving wolves, or pursued mile after mile by ever scarlet-tunicked Mounties in cold so intense their expectorations rattled on the ground in frozen drops.

I mentally crossed my fingers when we shoved the first long envelope across the post office counter. Log cabin living was so wonderful. If only we could solve our financial difficulties!

"When I compared myself with other men," wrote Thoreau, "it seems as if I were more favored by the gods than they."

I know exactly how he felt. Don't most city folk work hard all their lives in order to be able to retire some day to the uncrowded places? Aren't their weeks and months measured, in millions of instances, by the few days they can snatch from each harassed year for the brief free ecstasy of camping, fishing, hunting, or just plain rusticating?

Lonely? It was as if we were enjoying permanent vacations, and I didn't want to have to leave.

CHAPTER FIFTEEN

MAIL DAYS

We sent out more stories, trying to average one every seven days despite the distractions of approaching spring. All the while, we waited anxiously for replies. The weekly mail day assumed a new importance.

"Society is commonly too cheap," countered Thoreau when jibed about solitude. "We meet at very short intervals, not having had time to acquire any new value for each other. We meet at the post office, and at the sociable, and about the fireside every night. We live thick and in each other's way, and stumble over one another. I think we thus lose some respect for one another."

When Brad and I walked the six miles each way to Hudson Hope once a week, we appreciated those we met all the more for it. Each was a distinct character. The free lone life of the farther places, where the inhabitant is everything from his own private blacksmith to his personal doctor, leaves plenty of room for individuality.

Millions of workers are needed to keep the stupendous works of a great city functioning. A trifling chore on the part of each, however, is all that's necessary to maintain tremendous united achievements. In the city, for example, a citizen

109

can make a comfortable living for his family by working five days a week on an assembly line, giving a certain nut already atop a particular bolt a specified number of twists for year after year. With the money he thus earns, he is able to hire others to perform all the services necessary to his group's well-being.

In the bush, on the other hand, it is almost entirely up to the individual to keep the routine of daily living functioning. He can't reach for a telephone, and within a comparatively short time contract for the help of a skilled carpenter, plumber, electrician, baker, or even a taxi driver. He has to be a jack of all trades, depending upon his own resources. This is of course as it should be. The minutely organized city is too cramped to tolerate more than a handful who will not conform with the convenient patterns.

Where except in the wilderness, for instance, would anyone be more apt to display the ingenuity with which a former mail carrier between the then railhead of Rolla and Hudson Hope solved a thirsty problem? We've never met this particular driver, we'd like to add, and this is the one and only episode we know about him. The mail was carried in winter those days by horse and sleigh. The local mines had not yet done their part in effecting the present road and bridges, so the journey took several days even under favorable conditions.

Christmas was near. Inside one of the padlocked registered mail sacks could be heard the gurgle of whiskey and overproof rum, mailed on order to Hudson Hope sourdoughs from the provincial store. Every time the driver shifted the sacks, he was tormented by the provocative murmur. That night, when he brought the sacks inside his overnight cabin, an answer suggested itself.

There were a lot of disgruntled sourdoughs in Hudson Hope that particular holiday, but the sleigh wrangler wasn't feeling any pain. Nothing was ever proved against him, however. How could it be? No locks had been tampered with. Every seal still intact.

His solution had been to suspend the murmurous bag from a beam, place a wash basin beneath it, and then belabor the canvas with a billet of firewood.

Post Office Department precision is at a disadvantage at best in the farther places. The conscientious and excellent post master at Moberly Lake, Indian settlement two days by horse southward of Hudson Hope, would be as out of place in a city branch as the average Ottawa or Saint John clerk would be at Moberly. There was the day when a meticulous inspector thought he had uncovered a discrepancy in the Scotsman's account.

"No, the stamp money is all here," Harry Garbitt explained patiently, and he jerked a casual finger at a bundle of squirrel skins. "They're worth two-bits apiece."

"Do you mean you trade stamps for squirrel skins?" the inspector demanded with a note of awe, or so Harry interpreted it. "My goodness, I don't know what the department will say."

"Some Indians wanted stamps," Harry Garbitt explained patiently. "They didn't have any cash. Squirrel skins are worth two-bits. I pay that for them myself and trade them with Cuthill over at the Hope."

"My goodness," the inspector remarked again. "You trade squirrel pelts for stamps? Well, I guess the best thing will be not to say anything about it. I'm afraid it would confuse the almighty hell out of the Department."

One of the most moving scenes we've ever witnessed in connection with post offices took place when the one at Hudson Hope was located in Henry Stege's store. Vesta Gething, daughter of the erudite and brilliant Cornelius Morgan Gething who first promoted the local coal resources, has done her neighbors the favor of becoming post master for Hudson Hope. The handling of mail, therefore, is now all efficiency.

This episode took place early one morning when two old timers, Henry Stege and Fred Monteith, had charge of postal destinies hereabouts.

There was no response when some of us banged on the store door this particular morning, although it was common knowledge that Donald MacDougall had brought the mail in by pack horse the night before. Dennis Murphy and Joe Barkley were there from Beryl Prairie, and on hand, too, were Don MacDougall, King Gething, and also Harry Garbitt who wanted to get started back with the sacks for Moberly Lake. We finally went around to the side of the two-story log building. Some of the chinking was loose. We applied our eyes where it would do the most good.

The lemonish glare of an Aladdin Lamp revealed the bulky shapes of trader and settler, trousers pulled on with apparent haste over the long handled underwear that many bushmen wear the year around. Both old timers had bached alone in the wilderness for, as the expression went, as many years as a moose has ticks. Each, therefore, was in the habit of talking to himself. Henry Stege, as a matter of fact, often passed the quieter hours in his store by carrying on both sides of an animated two-way conversation.

"My, my, my, my, my," we could hear Fred muttering to himself this morning, as he sorted letters. "Too much mail, too much mail, too much mail."

Just then Henry emerged into view, carrying the big iron post-office key and still another padlocked sack. He glanced over his undersized glasses at Fred, and we could hear him scolding, also to himself, "Crazy, crazy, crazy, crazy, crazy."

Talking to one's self is a natural enough thing in the wilderness. I find myself doing it. King Gething, Brad informed me after an overnight trip to the latter's coal mining camp, carries the matter one step further and sings in his sleep. A number of our sourdough friends, including Dudley, make a habit of conversing with birds and squirrels. Bill Carter, with the characteristic independence of a former Mounted Police constable, enjoys the answering echo of his own voice.

Much unconscious humor is furnished for mail day conversations, of course, by the cheechako; the greenhorns, the tenderfeet, the dudes. One of them built his fire in the oven of a cook stove, not realizing evidently that there is such a refinement as a fire box. Another seriously asked Jim Holden, who was manager at the Bay at the time, "Which is warmer, sir? Snowshoes or moccasins?"

Sourdoughs, too, set the stage for many a chuckle. Where but in the unrestrained places, for instance, would one appreciate someone like affable Wyndham "Scotty" Smith who discovered the eight and one-half foot coal seam to which mine operator King Gething has now moved his camp.

"I can stick pins through my cheeks," the athletic young Scotsman was boasting good humoredly the other day to a group seated about the HB.C. store. "Doesn't bother me a bit."

"Yes," King nodded, "but you can't stand to have me put iodine on a cut."

Then there was the prospector on the upper Peace who slept with his head in a mulligan bucket after someone informed him that hungry pack rats sometimes nip a sleeper's ears. There was the time Dudley Shaw brewed the decoction of juniper berries for an ailing school teacher, who in the dark mistakenly grasped and drank a pan of dish water, made a hurried trip outdoors, and although never the wiser was cured anyway.

And there was the much lauded occasion when Fred Monteith, when the doorway to his new outhouse proved too narrow, ingeniously solved the problem with the least possible effort by whittling out enough of a curve to accommodate his rather prominent abdomen and thereafter sidling in and out of position.

Hudson Hope animals, too, develop personalities. One

dog, when he wanted to come inside the house during particularly cold spells, used to appear at the door and whine with a stick of firewood irresistibly in his mouth.

A white cat at King Gething's coal mine becomes as black as a marten when left alone for long, as occasionally happens when the mine is closed down for a few weeks. The mere appearance of human beings on the scene doesn't make any apparent difference in the cat's toilet, either. But when one stays as long as three days, the cat figures the visit is going to be permanent and starts to polish up.

Even some of the comparatively unspoiled sons of the forest disintegrate briefly into quaint characters under the pressure of the white man's example.

"Indian got good muscle," Dennis Michitee, son of a Beaver chief who lives two days north of Hudson Hope, was bragging to Brad just the other day. "Indian got muscle all the same moose."

"Fine," I heard Brad applaud understandingly. "Maybe you'll help me with the woodpile."

"Oh, no, no," handsome young Michitee gasped, recoiling with a smile from the ax handle Brad wryly extended. "Indian got soft hands."

"In one direction from my house there was a colony of muskrats in the river meadows. Under the grove of elms in the other horizon," Thoreau noted whimsically, "was a village of busy men, as curious to me as if they had been prairie dogs, each sitting at the mouth of its burrow or running over to a neighbor's to gossip. I went there frequently to observe their habits."

It took a month for a reply to reach Hudson Hope from the New York agent, although the intervening mail days were never dull. All the single sheet of paper said was, "Trying them out."

CHAPTER SIXTEEN

IS IT REALLY OVERRATED?

One attraction in coming to the woods to live, for us as well as Thoreau, was that we should have the opportunity of seeing Spring arrive. Even as we read Thoreau's enthusiasms, however, one of Ogden Nash's lines kept troubling me. Is Spring really a season much overrated for those already mated?

I didn't think so when we stood in a poplar grove one warm April morning and actually heard the leaves bursting open like popcorn. I didn't think so on afternoons we picked our way from snowbank to smoking snowbank through the dripping forest, alive now with the music of a thousand tinkling rills whose veins flowed with the blood of winter.

It was harder than ever to write with the frozen land coming alive all about us. Our fiction attempts continued, nevertheless. Conversations turned at odd moments to intricacies of plot and counterplot, in a way that often would have startled any casual passersby. We took turns with the typewriter and wrote in long hand the rest of the time. But after that initial note, no more was heard from the agent. Mail days were marked with exhilarating expectancy, then with repeated disappointment that more and more slowly became

115

moderated by the scene about us and by the possibility that no news might really be good news.

The river ice candled, its surface becoming rough with millions of short vertical spikes that crumbled crisply underfoot. Walking along the no longer slippery route had never been easier. We made it to Dudley's once by river in twenty-five minutes and on to Hudson Hope in an additional half hour.

Spring overrated? I didn't think so that morning when I watched the forms which thawing sand and clay assumed in flowing down the sides of the cutbanks enclosing the Peace River. Innumerable tiny streams of red, orange, brown, grey, and amber overlapped and interlaced. Occasional honeycombs of still frost-bound patches, glittering like stalactites, remained icily aloof. The streams gradually lost their individuality near the river's edge, broadening until they formed an almost flat surface which nevertheless was variously and gracefully shaded.

Some juvenile stories I'd sent out with great hopes arrived back promptly that particular mail day in the stamped self-addressed envelope I'd perhaps too conveniently enclosed. But the disappointment seemed trivial when we walked upriver with colored bands of the Aurora Polaris at our backs and moonlight and a gentle chinook beckoning us onward. No, Spring did not seem to be overrated.

Our brook, rushing over its icy sheath in expansive haste to leap the hundred musical feet to the swelling Peace River, sang carols to the Spring. The stream flooded suddenly on the afternoon of April eleventh with a muddy torrent that reached close to the cabin. If it had not been for brush and sweepers, Brad enthused, one could have poled a twelve-foot canoe up Bull Creek. The deluge filled depressions in the rottening Peace River ice with a turbid flow.

"Look at that, will you?" Brad said, standing by a miniature two-foot cascade above which we decided to dam a bathing pool. "This brook froze like a super layer cake."

Sure enough, I saw from the nearby cabin door, the ice was in many layers. The flowage surged over the topmost of these, cutting eventually to the next lamination and leaving the one above a mere shell that could be broken with the heel. As we frolicked like a pair of youngsters along the watercourse, Spring didn't seem overrated.

The going out of the ice in the Peace River, though, did seem to be a somewhat overrated phenomenon—at first, anyway. The river became dull and grimy, as the residue of winter snows melted and revealed the accumulated dust from cutbanks. More and more the ice candled, its surface becoming fibrous and brittle. Spring rains lay, damp and corroding, on its decaying splendor.

The pressure of awakening water increased inside the hidden channels. Parts of the reluctant sheath bulged, fractured, and became a jumbled mass of ice cakes. The spaces between these became frosted with white ice particles like snow which seemed to form a solid mass but through which one's foot instantly plunged.

The shore ice was engulfed by rising water which, like weak associates, started at once to corrupt it. For nearly three weeks afterwards, however, we could still pick our way up and down river once we had reached the solid core in the middle. We were exceedingly cautious if such adventures could be termed cautious. We never went alone, and we stayed roped a careful ten yards apart. We both carried longer poles than usual so that if we did break through, they'd more surely bridge the gap and give us purchase for getting out.

There was no need for going on the river, but it kept beckoning us. It promised fresh escapades and, besides, we could savor more of the awakening north by this road than by slowly picking our way overland. Sometimes new young riv-

ers, that cut channels atop the weakening ice, barred our
way. But we were always able to cross these on jammed ice
cakes or by precarious wading. The breath of danger kept
the game continually exciting.

Then one dusk a film of ice gave away beneath me in Box
Canyon. The narrow passage was high with a tremendous
confusion of ever crumbling and twisting cakes. I plunged
neck deep among huge ice blocks, conscious of Brad's fading
yell.

Dank air, as cold as water, engulfed me. It took a moment
before I could realize that I was still dry. Somewhat further
below was the growl of fiercely running water. The ice pack,
its booming strangely muffled now, seemed to be crushing
closer. Frantically I scrambled upward, hands desperate on
the slenderness of the pole that spanned the opening.

"Are you all right?" Brad demanded, white-faced.

"Yes, and . . . and I didn't even get wet."

"We've been behaving like a couple of kids." His voice, for
all its grimness, was even more unsteady than mine. "After
today, we're going to keep off this ice."

For the next week we watched the tormented ice break
free and then clog, crash loose once more then dam itself
anew. Box Canyon was the bottleneck. Finally, with an ex-
plosive surge that brought us running to the river bank on
April twenty-eighth, the Peace River hurled free. It became a dancing, blue-reflecting torrent in which glittering
white cakes spun, bobbed, and cavorted. A mighty roar
throbbed day and night. No, Spring did not seem one bit
overrated.

We picked our way overland past Box Canyon a week
later, then dropped to the river's edge. Why had we been
afraid the ice wouldn't support us, I wondered, sensing at
the same moment a smug glow because maybe we hadn't
been as foolhardy as I'd feared. Tremendous ice cakes, some
of them as tall as a Cape Ann cottage, had been left stranded

on the banks as evidence of how deeply the Peace had been frozen. Some of them dwindled there for weeks before completely melting.

The river swelled in the meantime. Now mingled with the jumping procession of ice came silt, brush, broken limbs, and finally great trees whose cumbersome roots twisted and dipped in such a fashion that they seemed to be daring us to climb aboard. The racing torrent was a never stilling phantasmagoria those early May days. I found myself delaying by the hour in the warm golden sunshine by the side of the cabin, fascinated by the possibilities of what each new moment might bring.

"No use trying to work indoors," Brad admitted finally, grabbing his ax.

In an hour he'd driven four sharpened lodgepole pine poles into the ground a few feet from where our waterfall arched over the cliff. He topped them with an old door to form a table. Two additional poles, each spiked horizontally across opposite pairs of uprights a foot below the table top, provided supports over which boards were nailed for seats.

Brad dedicated this new piece of furniture on the spot by bringing out our typewriter. Not to be surpassed, I served our one-dish supper of vegetables, meat, and dumplings outdoors that evening.

"Isn't this terrific?" he applauded, waving a fork about him. "When the flies do come, the breeze that follows the river will keep them pretty much away from here."

Brad, who'd spent some of his springs fishing for trout and Atlantic salmon in the dense pulpwood country of the northeast, was anticipating the fly season with trepidation; mostly, I suspected, insofar as I was concerned. He spoke so emotionally of dense black clouds of insects, so ravenous they could and sometimes did kill an unprotected human being, that I began to itch all over.

We'd been seeing a few large mosquitoes since the first of

May, the forerunners of the annual hatch according to Dudley. These giant insects were so sluggish that they were easily slapped while still contemplating where to begin operations. I picked up a couple of bottles of a colorless and almost odorless fly dope at the Bay. Brad, comparing it to the black and odiferous pine tar compounds that still stained some of his woolen shirts, shook a doubtful head. Nevertheless, with metropolitan innocence, I still refused to worry about anything as trivial as winged biters. If only we could get some good news about our stories, I thought I'd be able to accept any hardship this wilderness might offer.

Early one morning we were awakened by the thin distant cheeps of flying birds. Wings beat vaguely closer. Finally one of us made out a giant wavering V, hyphened against an amethyst sky.

"Swans," Brad said almost reverently, as we hurried outside. "Nearly 200 wild swans, coming North to nest."

Spellbound we stood warm together, intent on the great swift shapes until they chalked out of sight in the mountains upstream. Even afterwards I still seemed to be watching their strange instinctive passage until it became a dim atavistic shadow centuries deep in my consciousness.

"Brrrr," I realized finally, after the wild dimming clamor of the migrating flock had been long lost in the rush of the river and brook, "it's chilly this time of day, isn't it? But I couldn't possibly go back to bed. Could you, Brad?"

"We can sleep any time," he agreed. "Why waste this? It's mail day, anyway, Vena. We can get an early start to the Hope if you want."

"Then let's rustle some breakfast to chase away the goose pimples," I said happily. "I'll get a pail of water if you'll start the fire. Maybe we'll hear from those stories today."

He grasped a rustling handful of birchbark on our way back to the cabin. His other hand bent warmly around me. Spring didn't seem at all overrated.

CHAPTER SEVENTEEN

FOOD FOR THE FINDING

"Is that a moose or a bear?" Brad interrupted a few minutes later, as we sat beside our windows and ate steaming butter-yellowed oatmeal. He reached for his battered eight-power binoculars. "See that black thing up there by Box Canyon?"

I made out a dark blob in the water and mentally crossed my fingers. If it were a bear, its thick glossy fur would be in top condition after the long winter's sleep. Besides, bear were the only game animals it was now legal to shoot, and we needed meat.

"That's odd," my husband muttered. "Here, Vena, you take a look."

"It does look like a moose," I said doubtfully.

"It's a moose, all right," he agreed. "But why in the world should it be swimming backwards?"

That's what had been vaguely bothering me, too, I realized as I studied the object again. The animal was coming down the river in reverse. Was it a cow or bull, I wondered, seeking some reason for the strange behavior? The big head that kept glancing around was bare of antlers. Males have racks sometimes more than sixty inches wide in these mountains. Females with rare exceptions don't.

That didn't mean anything this time of year, of course, as bulls drop their antlers in winter. We'd found a number of spreads on the height of land a mile behind the cabin, on whose sunny prominences the gigantic animals like to lie that time of year, alert for sounds and odors of danger behind them and intent for any suspicious movement along the lower flat stretching to the river. I handed the glasses back to Brad.

"Hasn't that moose got something with it?" I asked him.

"Say, you're right," Brad ejaculated. "Yes! It's a cow with a new-born calf."

The cow, swinging her head occasionally to gauge her progress, was traveling backwards in such a way that the swollen current pressed the calf safely against her bulk. Moose are more at home in the water than any other large animal in the north, and this one was swimming high out of the flood and with little effort.

They landed on the rocky shore a few hundred yards above the cabin. The calf shivered in the sun. The mother dried it with a compassionate tongue, then turned to browsing in a patch of willows. The tiny tan creature stood uncertainly on its long colt-like legs then finally lay down against a warm boulder.

"Come on," Brad said, grabbing our Leica.

We hurried along the bank a hundred feet above the river, trying to get in position for a good picture. Lamb-like bleats drifted to our ears. Then, perhaps because one of the downward eddies of air told her of our presence, the cow stalked without apparent haste into the river. The small calf bleated piteously.

"Oh, is she going to desert it?" I almost cried.

The current floated the onyx black parent farther and farther out from shore. Then, desperately it seemed, the calf gave a final baa-a-a-a-a. It half-slid and half-stumbled into the brown torrent. There its gracelessness ended, although with the glasses we could see its nostrils distending frantically.

The cow moose swam upstream now, although the pace of the river here where it funneled out of Box Canyon was furious. The calf was driven in a moment securely against her again. I held my breath as they bobbed unscathed over a great reef on which in late summer, Dudley vowed, we could walk dry shod almost all the way across the Peace. Drifting, swinging erratically when gripped by eddies, they moved farther and farther away. We watched them land eventually on the south shore. They disappeared into the forest where bright patches of new leaves, more yellow than green, undulated like seaweed in an ocean of poplar tops.

"Who," I demanded, as we returned hand in hand to breakfast, "could ever seriously believe that Spring's overrated?"

Brad slung his light .250-3000 carbine over a shoulder when we set off down the river trail toward Hudson Hope.

"Maybe this is the day we'll get some bear steaks," he noted happily.

Brad had spied one scrawny article across river the evening before, although I hadn't seen it. All he could do was fire a shot well over its head in the chance that the confusing echo might send it swimming to our bank. This particular bruin merely took another drink, he said, raised on his hind legs for a casual look around, and scrambled unconcernedly back the way it had come. By the time I rushed out for a look, it had disappeared.

The carbine caught the bright eyes of Gene Boring when we encountered this homesteader and dude wrangler below Dudley's. The short, quiet-spoken redhead was looking over the bunch of horses that grazed the year around on the open hillsides about Hudson Hope.

"Guess my own cayuses wintered in good shape," Gene noted, indicating a bay and a sorrel. "They're not as fat as some I've got ranging over at Beryl Prairie, but the vetch and peavine will start picking them all up. Say, I'd sure like to deal you out of that gun some day."

"Well, I've got a .300, too, and I can only use one of them at a time," Brad said. "Customs would clear it all right, I suppose, after the duty was paid. Any bear around, Gene?"

"Seen one above town day before yesterday," Gene Boring nodded. "They're mostly gnawing jackpine bark now and drinking water. The bark cleans them out. They won't start putting on any lard for a while yet."

He'd been adjusting a rope around the neck of the red gelding, and now he slipped a half hitch onto its jaw. Grasping the mane with two hands, he swung onto the bare back. The horse made several halfhearted bucks, but the pressure of knees and rope straightened him out.

"Be seeing you all," Gene called with a wave of his broad brimmed hat. "Stop in when you get a chance."

The mail wasn't ready when we got to the post office. We chatted with Joe Barkley awhile, and then Joe disappeared with a brown-wrapped package into the Gething house. When he came out, Mr. Gething appeared, too, and smilingly advanced toward us.

Neil Gething, the handsome and robust head of that mining family, insisted hospitably that we have tea with him while the mail was being sorted. Beyond the closed door across from the humming kitchen range we could hear his daughter, Vesta, sorting the envelopes and bundles Les Bazeley had just brought from Fort St. John in a dozen grey sacks.

"Joe Barkley says you two may be visiting Clara and him soon out at Beryl Prairie," Mr. Gething noted by way of conversation, putting fresh wood in the stove and moving a teakettle and a cracked white teapot forward.

"Yes, he just invited us," Brad nodded.

"You'll enjoy yourself. They're both very nice. We've some land out that way, too. You know, Beryl Prairie was named after my granddaughter, Beryl Gething."

He put cups, plates, silverware, bread, jam, and meat on the table. Then he unwrapped the brown package that I'd just seen Joe Barkley carrying. It proved to contain butter. I looked around with a woman's curiosity. Mr. Gething smiled when he saw me sniff appreciatively at the spicy odor emanating from the white teapot.

"That's my special tea." Mr. Gething beamed with hospitality. "It's a sort of spring tonic, too. Would you and Brad like to try some?"

Noting Mr. Gething's healthy countenance, serene and somehow youthfully radiant beneath a frosted thatch of snow white hair, I rapidly decided that any special tea of his might be a good thing to try. Without any excess weight, Mr. Gething was squarely and ruggedly built, and we knew that although he was over eighty years old he still worked from dawn to dusk at things he enjoyed doing. He smiled friendily now, as he filled our cups with a pale greenish fluid.

"One drinks it like Chinese tea," he suggested. "Personally, I like mine with milk and a little sugar."

So did I. Brad, who prefers his orange pekoe black, sipped his portion unadulterated and then experimentally with evaporated milk and a teaspoon of sugar. He also preferred it the latter way.

"Besides being tasty, yarrow tea cleanses the kidneys," Mr. Gething mentioned with scientific detachment. "I brew it from yarrow blossoms. You'll find them here the year around, but I usually gather a few paper bags full every fall and hang them from a rafter to dry. They're those flat-topped blooms, composed of dozens of little white flowers, that one sees on single green stems a foot or two high. But you both know what yarrow is, of course."

"Isn't that some right outside this window?" When he nodded, I went on with increasing interest, "We've heard that a lot of edibles grow wild up here, Mr. Gething."

"Yes, that's right," Mr. Gething agreed in a tone that seemed to take for granted that all three of us understood such matters. "There's several different so-called teas, as you know. Plain ordinary dandelion roots belong to the chickory family. When dried and roasted in the oven, they make a creditable coffee substitute. There's even a lot of so-termed wild tobaccos that trappers and prospectors sometimes smoke."

"I've heard Dudley talk about stuffing his pipe full of kinnikinic," Brad agreed.

"That's right," Mr. Gething smiled with growing enthusiasm. "You know, of course, that what most folks around here refer to as kinnikinic isn't that at all. It's really the shredded inner bark of the flowering dogwood which a lot of people call red willow. Kinnikinic is actually a little plant, as you know. It's what covers that particularly green hillside right above town, see? It's all over the slopes at the head of Bull Creek, too.

"Oh, so that's what that is," Brad said.

"That's right," Mr. Gething nodded. "Real kinnikinic was used so much as a tobacco substitute, around the Ohio River for instance, that whenever someone crammed any sort of wild leaves or bark into his pipe, he automatically thought of the mixture as kinnikinic."

"Dudley says he's smoked dried fireweed leaves, too," Brad put in. "He said that once he even broke up an old pipe and smoked that."

Mr. Gething nodded his white head. Labrador tea, the curling rusty-bottomed leaves of the short perennial shrub we'd noticed in muskegs, is another favorite tobacco substitute, he said. So in a pinch was regular Chinese tea, this being the reason why some bushmen refused to pack space-saving compressed tea. Farther north, dried and cut leaves of the ground cranberry were particularly popular. As a matter of fact, Mr. Gething chuckled, Bill Carter often asserted that the worst thing he had ever smoked was tobacco.

The three of us talked and laughed until Brad finally had to admit reluctantly we'd better do our shopping at the Hudson's Bay Company if we were going to be able to start for home as soon as the mail was distributed.

"Aren't a lot of wild things coming up now that are good to eat, Mr. Gething?" I asked almost desperately. "We've heard about some of them, but I'm not sure what they look like."

"Yes, the species we have here in the northwest do vary from those around Boston," Mr. Gething agreed with so much diplomacy that I felt almost wise. "I've got to go look at my horses. Hear the bells over there by the barn? If you don't have to go to the Bay, too, Mrs. Angier, why don't you walk along? We'll see quite a few greens that grow wild up by your cabin, too."

What I learned that afternoon made me feel a little better as we trudged homeward through the long northern twilight. No check had dropped out of the long-awaited envelope from New York. Instead, there had been a single sheet of paper and, above the agent's printed initials, only two words: "No bites."

"No blizzards," Brad uttered discouragedly. "No man-eating wolves. No saliva freezing before it hits the ground. No sales. I guess folks are too accustomed to exaggerations about the North to want to read stories that are halfway true to life."

"We ought to surprise them with some articles that are all the way true," I grumbled, kicking at a root. Pain jarred my foot, and then I forgot all about it. "That's it, Brad! Let's really try some practical, down-to-earth articles."

"About blizzards that aren't," he muttered, "and attacking wolves that don't?"

"Later, maybe," I thought aloud. "Why not start with subjects in which everyone had some first-hand interest. Mr. Gething was telling me after you left that there are actually tastier, more nourishing foods growing free throughout North America than one can buy at any price in the average city market."

"How's that?" Brad asked, interested.

"He explained that a lot of wild greens thrive unrecognized within the limits of even such big cities as New York and Boston," I recounted. "Well, we've both read how aging quickly destroys some of the vitamins present in leafy foods. So freshly gathered wild greens would have more Vitamin C than any store vegetables, wouldn't they?"

"Yes," Brad said slowly, stopping and regarding me. "That's right, isn't it?"

"Of course, it is. Oh, he told me lots of things, and he pointed out nearly a dozen different foods. I've brought along samples. Why don't we learn all we can about them and do an article on that?"

"It sounds all right," Brad admitted, shifting the strap of his carbine.

"It is all right," I echoed with deliberate enthusiasm. "Besides, look at the fun we'll have eating all those fresh wild things. And think of the money we can save."

Looking downriver along trail toward Hudson Hope.

Looking upriver from in front of cabin.

CHAPTER EIGHTEEN

BEAR WITH GOLDEN PAWS

Nothing was left of the sun but a splash of copper in the darkening purple of the turgid Peace River. We'd stopped in a steep-walled coulee where a spring at Dudley Shaw's western boundary made a morass of the trail. A low quavering cry burst from a nearby hollow.

"Easy," Brad cautioned, suddenly alert. "That sounds like a young mus-kwa."

The noise was not unlike the wailing of a punished child. The animal making the racket was, I realized, not at all dangerous. Yet its four-legged parent could break a horse's neck with one blow.

"See," my husband motioned quietly enough, although his carbine was no longer slung over a casual shoulder, "there it is. Easy now, honey. Don't make any sudden moves."

A little bear, brown and scrawny as a monkey, was clawing its way up a young spruce. The small conifer arched beneath his weight. Then it broke with a loud snap. The cub sprawled on its back in a prickly clump of blue-berried juniper. Its shrieks and howls increased. Then I saw a similar tiny shape roll toward it. We had walked to within fifteen yards of twin cubs.

I'd never seen a bear before outside of the zoo at Franklin

Park and another I'd visited in Antwerp. I'd particularly never seen a cub, and here were two of them. They were so cute. I guess I just froze there open-mouthed.

The cubs weren't like the fat cuddly little creatures I'd seen pictured on calendars, though. They were a lot longer than they were round. They seemed mostly bones and skin, in fact, spared from nakedness only by a sparse bristle of hair. Born while their mother drowsed in the torpor of hibernation, they'd snuggled close to her warmth and nursed spasmodically while she continued to sleep in her dark leaf-softened den.

Baby bears, incongruously enough, are among the smallest and most helpless of wilderness creatures. These had been scarcely larger than kittens at birth. Now each was nearly a foot long. They probably hadn't been outside in the exciting open world for more than a few days, and in all likelihood their mother had parked them here while she went in search of food. Already the two were wrestling together again, apparently forgetting we were near.

"Easy," Brad was saying. One hand was firm on my arm while the other, I was dimly aware, was keeping the gun barrel partially raised. "Everything's going to be all right. The mother's coming, but everything's going to be all right."

I'd been so fascinated by the tiny cubs that, for what could not have been more than the fraction of a minute, I'd forgotten everything else. Now I realized that for moments the noise of crashing brush had been registering dully in my consciousness. I remembered, also with sudden propeller-fast clarity, what I'd been warned was the most dangerous thing anyone could do in these woods. It was to get between a mother bear and her baby.

Then another fear sent a chill spasm, followed by the prickle of enervating heat, flooding up my backbone. Black bears as a species varied in color here, I knew, from cinnamon to dark onyx. But there were unpredictable grizzlies in these mountains, too, and these were commonly brownish. What were these cubs? I looked about me in sudden panic. Why didn't we flee somewhere, anywhere? The grip tightened on my arm.

"It's too late to do anything but sit tight," Brad was assuring me, and an unnatural calm stripped his words and left them stark. "Just take it easy. You've seen dogs chasing moving automobiles, but you never saw one bite a parked car. We'll be all right."

The crashing came frighteningly nearer. Then it stopped. The hold on my arm slackened, as both hands now whitened on the gun. A bulking shadow loomed dark not fifty yards away. It was above us in the coulee made by years of erosion by the spring's overflow, and I realized that the animal would have to pass by us to reach the cubs.

"Take it easy, Old Bruin," Brad was saying, and all of a sudden I realized he wasn't trying to be humorous. His voice, despite the almost absurd words, was quiet and somehow reassuring. I remembered one thing he'd told me about wild beasts. If one of them confronts you in the course of ordinary events, the best thing to do is to talk calmly and not make any sudden moves. "See, Old Bruin, we're not harming your babies."

One of the cubs bawled again. The massive bear's incongruently tiny eyes fixed on it suspiciously. Then they gleamed back at us. The two cubs started to frolic again. Reluctant to move away from where she could evaluate the scene, she edged cautiously along the slanting bank opposite us, not fifty feet away. In this manner she reached the cubs.

She touched noses inquiringly, compassionately, exuberantly with both. Suddenly I felt as I had when we'd first witnessed the full-dress magnificence of the Northern Lights. Once more it was as if we were being admitted behind the scenes of nature's drama of unquenchable vitality, and I had to wink back the tears.

"Oh, the dear things," I heard myself breathe.

I was still intent, but with a new instinct now that bore nothing of fear. The mother bear ambled away with every appearance of casualness, as if not wanting to violate what she, too, seemed to respect as a moment of truce. Then, as if this act had become so melodramatic that the Supreme Director realized it needed the relief of comedy, the cubs recommenced playing. The mother bear hesitated, stopped, waited, and then with an air not unlike that of an exasperated human matron waddled back.

A final shaft of daylight shone on her saucer-like paws as she turned. They seemed for an instant to be made of gold. The cubs didn't stop cavorting, even when she reached them. You should have seen the spanking she gave the nearer one with her left paw. Both skinny little fellows scampered obediently after her then, their raucous bawling once more filling the green wilderness.

"Ah hah," Brad chuckled exultantly, treating me as disrespectfully before drawing me within the clasp of his free arm. "And let that be a warning to you."

I felt myself tremble, as if the brink of terror had not been far away. But the emotion was greater than that, although even in my own mind I could not analyze it, and I buried my face in the smoke-keen roughness of his woolen shirt. The ecstasy of sweet Spring seemed almost overpoweringly close, as the last noise of the now hurrying bears became lost in the murmur of the swollen river.

"Did you see that bear's paws?" I asked two miles later, when we crossed the brook to our cabin. "They seemed golden. Maybe that's a sign I should pan for gold near there when the river gets low enough."

"Maybe seeing that bear tonight," Brad said more practically, "is a sign I'd better start hunting in earnest if we're going to collect an unattached young bruin to go with those wild vegetables you're going to find."

"I suppose it's all right," I said at last.

"Sure, it is," he nodded quietly. "We need meat to live."

The honking of great Canada geese, flying low up the river, peopled the woods with the sound of a larger life as Brad fumbled for our latchstring. We made out the dim silhouettes and heard the swish of wings. Then as Brad's packsack clumped on the floor and a match snapped into flame against his thumb nail, I took our copy of Thoreau's *Walden* from its shelf.

"As it grew darker," I read aloud in the sudden carbon-rich flare of lamplight, "I was startled by the honking of geese flying low over the woods, like weary travelers getting in late from Southern lakes and indulging at last in unrestrained complaint and mutual consolation. Standing at my door, I could hear the rush of their wings. I came in, and shut the door, and spent my first spring night in the woods."

"Well," Brad said, "Spring's a few weeks later this far north, that's all."

The change from storm and winter to serene and mild weather, from dark and sluggish hours to bright and elastic ones, was still a memorable crisis which all nature proclaimed. The alteration was seemingly instantaneous. Chinooks gentled a frosty world in our case, and then abruptly became spring. Ice was still present. Additional snow wafted down from time to time to whiten the still deep drifts in the forest beyond. But there was no more winter.

A single gentle rain made the grass along the bare slopes and the river bank many shades greener. So our prospects brighten on the influx of better thoughts, philosophized Thoreau.

We should be blessed if we lived in the present always, and took advantage of every accident that befell us—like the grass which confesses the influence of the slightest dew—

and did not spend our time in atoning for the neglect of past opportunities. Many of us loiter in winter, he noted, when it is already Spring.

"Yesterday is ashes, tomorrow wood," the Indians phrase it. "Only today does the fire burn brightly."

The next morning, while Brad went hunting upriver, I took to the bush in search of wild edibles. The season wasn't as advanced here as on the cleared flat where sprawled the log cabins of Hudson Hope. I did have some success, though.

My prize find was a large patch of nettles. I remembered when my cousins and I had blundered barelegged among some while playing tag on my uncle's farm, and I'd never considered the language-provoking plant in terms of food. Mr. Gething had assured me otherwise. I was still doubtful, however, as I dutifully slipped on gloves and went to work with knife and oilskin bag.

Maybe that was why I felt like a bystander that evening when my husband sauntered toward the cabin with a new fervency in his stride. He tried to keep his voice casual. Yet he couldn't eliminate from the tones a certain atavistic excitement—a throwback, dulled by civilization but none the less vital for all that—when he mentioned that the meat of a certain tender two-year-old bruin now hung in our cache.

I felt like an onlooker, that is, until Brad in turn went into ecstasies about the wild fruits and vegetables I served with at least equal nonchalance along with the broiled bear liver.

The dark green nettle tops were ready for a crowning pat of butter a minute after being dropped into boiling salted water. Highbush cranberries and wild rose hips, stewed with a little sugar, were our dessert that supper.

"Darling, do you know what this means?" Brad asked. Some moments in a lifetime stand out, and I'll never forget how he pulled me to his lap in a way that was almost comradely but not quite. "It doesn't make so much difference now that we're not drawing down city pay checks. You've proved we can live off the country."

"We've both proved it," I corrected. "Tomorrow we begin preserving what meat we can't use right away. Nothing's going to waste in this family."

CHAPTER NINETEEN

LIVING OFF THE COUNTRY

We had two new motives from then on. One was to subsist as much as possible on foods the wilderness so pleasantly offered. The other was to learn what we could of wild edibles so that we might compress that knowledge into a salable article.

We needed food, and we needed money. Our fiction, perhaps because the first-hand impressions we incorporated in it had little of the lupine savagery and icy peril of most of the so-called northern stories we read, was still not selling. What difference did it make if the U. S. Weather Bureau bore out the fact that it actually gets colder in popular Yellowstone National Park than at Barrow on Alaska's northernmost tip? What did it matter if 100° in the shade has been recorded at Fort Yukon, north of the Arctic Circle?

What if more snow does fall in Chicago during an average winter than along much of the Alaska Highway? What if blizzards are actually unknown in many northern sections including Hudson Hope? What if even in the refrigerated interior of Alaska and the Yukon, thermometers drop little if any lower than in the beautiful states of Montana and Wyoming. What if elsewhere they're surprisingly higher?

136

The average January temperature of such a rightfully great American city as Minneapolis runs some dozen degrees below zero. Compare that to such above-zero January averages in Alaska as 22° in Seward, 27° in Juneau, 29° in Wrangell, and 32° in Ketchikan which incidentally is south of us. But what did that matter if magazine readers wanted to picture their North as an inert, silent land of eternal ice and snow? If we were going to make any money writing, we decided, perhaps our best bet would be to try something factual.

Some have asked us if there weren't fur-bearing animals about our cabin? Yes, there were beaver, fisher, lynx, fox, coyote, weasel, cougar, skunk, wolverine, muskrat, and of course wolves. There was a poor grade of mink. There was the finest marten in the world, with a glossy and luxuriant fur sold by some retailers as Hudson Bay Sable. Even the chattering little red squirrel was worth from a quarter to seventy-five cents, depending on market fluctuations. Some trappers, armed with the inevitable .22 rifle with which they kill everything including moose and grizzly, case and bundle two thousand or so of the tiny pelts each year.

But one doesn't head just anywhere in the North Woods and start trapping. In British Columbia, for example, there are registered trap lines. Every square foot of the country is divided into specific if sometimes loosely defined areas. Dudley Shaw, for example, had the exclusive right to trap in the woods about our cabin. My catching a fisher in our yard would have been, in addition to a violation of law and custom, the same as stealing one hundred dollars from Dudley's pocket.

"We might as well get at that bear meat before we do anything else," Brad suggested the next morning.

"Shall we smoke it?" I asked vaguely.

"No, that would take days," he demurred. "Let's try the

receipt I copied from that Hornaday book the library sent us. Then the meat will be cured without any more work in about a month. We can eat it then without cooking if we want. In fact, the book says it's better that way."

"Well, maybe," I rejoindered doubtfully, starting to get things ready.

Brad cut the fibrous red meat into lengths about the size of his forearm, following the membranous divisions among the muscles whenever possible. Meaty bones, the tastiest part of any animal, I dropped into a pot for mulligan along with scraps. We saved out some roasts and steaks, too. We pulled what we could of shielding membrane off the rest and rolled the pieces in a readily clinging mixture composed of three pounds of table salt, four tablespoons of allspice, and five tablespoons of black pepper.

Brad pierced the shorter chunks, inserting string, and tied them from a wire angled across the inside of our cache. The longer strips he merely draped across the wire. We put down some old newspaper to keep the drippings off the floor, left the door and shaded windows ajar to insure a cool influx of dry air, and wondered if we could wait a whole month to sample the results of our first experiment in curing meat.

We tacked up the hide with its fur against the outer southern wall of the cache where, protected from any rain by the eaves, it would sun-tan. A pair of bright-eyed Canada jays immediately volunteered their aid, by pecking at what flesh had not been entirely scraped off.

"That should feel nice and warm under your feet next winter," Brad noted as we went to wash in the brook, cold water doing a better initial job than warm after one has been handling any large amount of fresh meat. "Now let's see what else the wilderness has to offer."

Searching for new foods proved to be fun. Willow shoots, I found, made a concoction that my husband affirmed he couldn't distinguish from celery soup. Gathering dandelion greens took me back to girlhood days when I used to cling to my father's hand along some of the slippier portions of the slope by our suburban Boston home, where the yellow blossoms first peeked out in the spring.

Pigweed proved to be one of the most delicately flavored greens we have, particularly when I served it as "amaranth" as it's also known. Some of the common wild foods are plagued by psychological handicaps, similar to that which bans roast muskrat from many a table. The succulent dark meat of the little water animal is actually hard to equal—especially when it's sliced, moist and steaming from the oven, as musquash or swamp rabbit.

Enough new pigweed kept coming up, so that I always seemed able to find tender new plants. This would continue, Mr. Gething had assured me, until frost-withering fall. Nor are the leaves and stalks of the widely scattered weed its only taste-tempting components, he said. The dried seeds make an excellent cereal. Before Indians began listening to radio serials and buying oatmeal, some of them used to put up huge quantities each year. We found oatmeal a lot less work, too. But we did appreciate the pumpernickel complexion the seeds gave to what Brad, in the continued absence of any bread-making success on my part, began to call, "That banal bane of the backwoods—bannock."

Old timers, when they learned we were interested, began to introduce us to additional wild foods. Almost every sourdough has one or two favorites, we found, cussing as weeds other edibles that would have made Epicurus himself smack an appreciative lip.

A grub-stretching trick of sourdough chefs, Ted Boynton volunteered, is the doctoring of flour until it is as much as one-third dried and powdered caribou moss.

"I did it once myself on a pinch," he chuckled, "and the dudes never noticed the difference."

This is similar to the occasional practice of British Colum-

bia Indians who, when supplies become low, augment dwindling flour stores with the dried and pulverized inner bark of
such trees as the poplar, birch and jackpine.

Dick Hamilton, a retired prospector and trapper, sent us
down some bread that he went to the trouble of making from
straight jackpine flour cooked with bear fat. He'd been careful to cut the bark only from the sunny side of the tree, he assured us. Since the laxative bark of this conifer is one of the
first feasts that bruins seek after hibernation, the combina-
tion did not seem at all inappropriate. I wouldn't have
missed the opportunity of sampling the bread for anything,
but I didn't crave any second helpings. The dryness and flat-
ness of the food was reminiscent of hardtack. At least, that's
how Brad described it, finishing the loaf by himself. I've
never eaten hardtack.

"Have you tried vetch or peavine yet?" Joe Barkley asked
when we met him down at the Hope again on another otherwise profitless mail day. "They're both species of wild peas.
They're the main reason the horses grazing out on Beryl
Prairie are so dingdanged fat."

"Why don't you come out to visit us and see for yourselves?" Clara, his trim little wife whom I liked at once, invited us. "You could even borrow a couple of horses and ride
over to Chinaman Lake if you wanted."

"That's right," Joe echoed, and when his bony good-
humored face lighted in a smile, one knew he wasn't just putting it on. "As a matter of fact, Gene Boring's got a couple of
well broken cayuses ranging out our way that he said you
could use any time. I reckon you'd find plenty of those wild
foods around that lake."

"Thanks an awful lot," I said appreciatively, and I looked
at Brad. "We'll certainly try to get over that way soon."

"If that's really okay about the horses," Brad put in, "what
say we make it some day next week? That Chinaman Lake

trip sounds like just what we need to round off an article we're working on."

"Wonderful," Clara enthused, and Joe echoed, "Sure, it's all right about the cayuses. You could use a couple of ours if it wasn't. They're just not as gentle, that's all."

We picked some vetch and peavine flowers on the way back upriver that evening. The white buds of the peavine proved to be exceedingly sweet. The purple blooms of vetch had more the flatter taste of garden peas. The seeds, although small, made delicious cooked peas when we tried them later. I found I liked to eat them raw, too, when out walking. The tender leaves made nutritious greens, both raw and boiled, alone and in salads and mulligans.

Another wild vegetable that's tasty when boiled with meat is rock tripe. This lichen grows on rocks throughout most of the United States and Canada in small and often pitted discs that, except for the darker color, look like upcurling dry lettuce leaves rooted by their middles. When Sir John Franklin and his three shiploads of men were lost in the Arctic, some stayed alive for weeks on rock tripe.

This vegetable, I discovered, required considerable washing to rid it of sand and grit. The taste was improved if it was roasted in a pan or in the oven before going into the soup, which it thickened to the consistency of gumbo and to which it imparted a somewhat bland tapioca-like flavor.

The reddish bark from the roots of the birch tree made a pleasant enough tea when dropped into boiling water, then set off the fire in the usual fashion to steep for five minutes. Fresh young twig tips will also serve, we found. We tried some of the nourishing inner bark, too, which has been eaten by Indians for centuries. It proved to be unexpectedly sweet.

Once more I remembered the sugar maples of New England. My mouth watered, as I recalled riding into a moist sunny grove behind yoked oxen and eating a golden sticky patch of boiled syrup hardened top a snowdrift.

"No, we don't have any maples here. Ghastly," Dudley had told me regretfully the previous mail day, eyes sparkling humorously behind their heavy spectacles. "We have birch trees, though."

"I know," I replied somewhat vaguely, "but I was thinking of maple syrup."

"I'll give you a receipt for making a noble syrup you can't tell from maple syrup," Dudley promised. "You use ordinary sugar and potatoes. But birch syrup you can get here in copious amounts. Heavenly concoction. It'll cheer Brad up vastly."

"Oh, will you show me how?"

"I'll stow a gimlet in my pack when I prowl up that way the first of the week to retrieve a couple of traps that got frozen in," Dudley agreed. "Noble lap, birch syrup is. Glorious on flippers."

"He means flappers," Brad chuckled.

"Sourdough pancakes," I nodded. "We'll have a batch to dedicate the new syrup."

Dudley told me to ready some containers. Lard pails would do, he said, or I could attach some wire bails through nail holes punched in the tops of several tomato cans. He beamed approval when he arrived early Tuesday morning. The improvised sap buckets, suspended on nails driven above the small holes Dudley bored with his gimlet, caught a dripping flow of watery fluid.

"You'd better ramble out this way regularly to see these don't overflow," Dudley cautioned. "Keep the emptied sap simmering cheerfully on the back of the stove. Tons of steam have to come off."

"Will it hurt the trees any?" I asked anxiously.

"No, no," Dudley said reassuringly. "The plunder will begin to bog down when the day cools, anyway. Then we'll whittle out pegs and drive them in to close the blinking holes. Everything will be noble."

Everything was, especially the birch syrup. It wasn't as thick as it might have been, even after all that boiling. There was a distressingly small amount of it, too. But what remained from the day's work was sweet, spicy, and poignantly delicious. Was there any limit to what these North Woods could furnish?

CHAPTER TWENTY

THE MOUNTAIN LAKE

"I learned from my experience that it cost incredibly little trouble to obtain one's necessary food," Thoreau stated, "and that a man may use as simple a diet as the animals and yet retain health and strength."

Spring made us restless. I suppose that, abetting as it did an ambition to get additional background material with which to round off our article on wild foods, was why we decided to camp out a few days and really live off the country. All we took besides some extra clothing was a light eiderdown, a small ax, and part of our nested cooking outfit.

We walked through the greening woods, heading generally northwest by compass and picking the easiest going. We struck the portage trail near its turnoff northward to Beryl Prairie. Bullhead Mountain, visible from the Alaska Highway and stretches of the Peace River but not from Hudson Hope nor our cabin, reached its crest five miles obliquely ahead to our left. Ahead almost as obliquely to our right, the Butler Range extended out of sight in a succession of heightening ridges that arrowed nearly due north.

The Peace River had flowed during pre-glacial centuries through the gap between Bullhead and the southern extrem-

Brad with packdog.

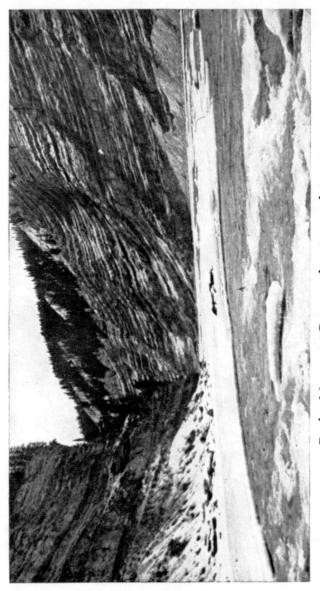

Rocky Mountain Canyon showing coal seams.

Dudley Shaw.

Mr. Gething.

Ted Boynton, Marion Cuthill, Brad and Dudley Shaw.

Vena heating the kettle.

ity of the Butler Range. Then the melting glacier had choked that pass with earth and stones that Dr. F. H. McLearn and other visiting geologists referred to as terminal moraine. This had forced the river to cut, past where our cabin now stood, a rough 22-mile passage that was nearly twice the length of the earlier route.

The resulting Rocky Mountain Canyon, where the water drops a roisterous 270 feet before calming again near Hudson Hope, is one of the few remaining lengths among the world's great rivers that has never been run by any boatman. Even the Grand Canyon of the Colorado has been singly and jointly conquered. No one had even walked through Rocky Mountain Canyon for its entire length, as far as we could learn, except for a small survey party which with the Gething's help managed to get up the ice one particularly favorable winter with ropes and dogs. Maybe, I thought now— exhilarated on the eve of this new adventure in living—Brad and I might be able to traverse it one way or another some day soon.

Clara and Joe Barkley were hungry for visitors, and as we were surely more eager for company than they, the four of us talked late into the night. Like Thoreau, Brad and I had found we "love society as much as most," and here was a particularly fine brand of it.

The horses were already in the corral. We heard them stamping during the night, and once when I slipped over for a look, the lighter colored of the two had put his head inquiringly over the bars and let me stroke his sleek neck.

"This here grey gelding is Cloud," Joe said in the early mistiness of the next morning. The horse I'd petted the night before pulled briefly against the halter rope I was holding when Joe swung on a saddle. "The little beggar is so smart he's lazy. He's got a nice smooth lope that he'll ease into, though, if you show him you're boss. . . ."

"Or if Chinook—that's this sorrel mare—gets too far ahead," Clara interrupted with a laugh. "Cloud enjoys feminine companionship."

"Didn't I say he was smart?" Joe responded, giving the grey belly a crisp good-natured slap. Cloud breathed out an audible lungful of air he'd been holding in reserve as insurance against the saddle's being cinched too tightly according to his standards. Joe drew the latigo up two more notches. "He's the gentlest dingdanged cayuse I ever saw, too. I imagine maybe you'll want to ride him, won't you, Vena?"

There was the sharpness of wood smoke and the not unpleasant odor of stirring cattle. The Butler Range was a sun-gilded purple through the nearby greenness of lodgepole pine. Joe glanced back at me inquiringly, as he started to help Brad ready the trim-legged sorrel mare who danced away theatrically, with a white show of eyes, as a blanket flopped across her glossy red back. Rubbing Cloud's soft inquisitive nose, I nodded.

Yellow sunshine was buttering the heat-toasted trail when, after final convivial cups of tea, we headed toward the lake. Spruce grouse exploded almost from beneath the cayuses' feet. It was fun to be riding horses, with all our supplies for the next few days tied with what I was sure must be swashbuckling casualness behind the cantles of our saddles. We swung westward toward the mountains at Ed Brouillette's and northward again, a half-mile further along, at Jessie and Dennis Murphy's where we ran into a brief patch of snow. Gunnar Johnson was there, fondling a litter of the five cutest husky pups I'd ever seen. We couldn't resist taking pictures and then, of course, came the pleasant ritual of tea.

"You can't miss the trail," Dennis assured us, opening the two gates that let us through his barnyard which bisected the thoroughfare. "You'll cross Lynx Creek at the foot of the hill here, and you'll have to wade another creek a few miles further along where there's an overnight cabin I built. After that, the trail splits. You'll see where Joe Barkley took the right hand turn all winter with freight for Teddy Green. You keep going west up into the mountains."

"Be sure to stop in on the way back," Jessie called hospitably, and Gunnar Johnson with some embarrassment tried to head off the five puppies who all streamed yapping at the heels of the horses.

Chinaman Lake, said to be named phonetically after an Indian whose cross-denoted grave some averred was the one we noticed at the left of the trail a short distance beyond the second ford, was so nestled in the slopes of the abrupt Butler Range that Spring seemed to be just arriving here although the date was already May.

"Look at that snow, will you?" Brad demanded, neck reining Chinook around a drift that bulged high at a spot where the banks of the Peace River were blue in the distance.

"It's just like turning back a page in a calendar, isn't it?" I chortled delightedly.

"Yes," he said, but mixed with appreciation was a certain note of direness. "I hope it doesn't knock our plans of living off the country sky-high."

The meaning of anxiety did not register at once. The sight of the small mountain lake framed before us, was reminding me too potently of Thoreau's description of his own Walden Pond.

"A forest mirror," he had called it and could, I thought now, have no more perfectly described this. "It is a mirror which no stone can crack, whose quicksilver will never wear off, whose gilding Nature continually repairs—a mirror which retains no breath that is breathed upon it, but sends it out to float as clouds high above its bosom and be reflected in its bosom still."

The snow piles dwindled as we trotted onto the sun-brightened flat at the north end of the lake. Among the drifts were verdant patches at which Cloud started to nibble when I swung, as gracefully as possible, to the budding ground.

"Well, there'll be enough grazing, anyway," Brad allowed, dismounting, too. "Say, isn't that a patch of nettles over by that cabin? Ouch, doggone it. It sure is. We'll make out, I guess. Well, do we bunk in the cabin, or do we camp out?"

"Oh, let's not go indoors!"

He seemed relieved, as he unsaddled Cloud and Chinook. We picketed them nearby by thirty-foot lengths of rope, fastened to a forefoot of each by a non-jamming bowline knot and then anchored to convenient saplings. The sun was causing the compact masses of neve to steam and the awakening woodlands to emit pleasant pungencies. With a grin that wouldn't seem to come off, Brad helped me gather fuel. Then we filled a teakettle and pot from a hole he broke with a heel in the honeycombed ice that still lay over this extremity of Chinaman Lake.

"I'll build us a browse bed later on," he promised. "Right now, I'd better see if I can collect some grouse for dinner."

"Oh, we forgot our .22," I gasped.

"No, we didn't," he grinned. "I left it behind on purpose. It wasn't in the rules. Anyway, all I should need for this job are a few stones. These fowl are so stupid that some of them will even let a lost man reach up with a dead limb and knock them off a branch."

When he returned less than a half hour later, though, he carried two dusky white birds of a species I'd never seen before.

"Ptarmigan cocks," he identified. "They're in the process of darkening up, like the varying hares around here, after being white all winter. We sure are going to make out all right. How did you do with vegetables, Vena?"

"We'll make out," I smiled.

Young fireweed stalks rival asparagus, we found. I cut the

new green shoots into mouth-sized sections and boiled them in a small amount of water until tender. The tops and leaves of wild mustard had a clean, slightly bitter delicacy. Prickly lettuce soon lost its sting in bubbling water. Miners lettuce retained its crisp tastiness when dropped into a scanty amount of steaming water which was immediately set off the fire to cool.

Besides containing important minerals, we had learned, wild vegetables are rich in such vitamins as A, B, C, E, G, K, and niacin. If merely for this reason, they should be cooked only until tender and in as little fluid as possible. Greens, the Hudson's Bay Company advises its fur traders, may often be lifted directly from the rinse to the saucepan and prepared without additional liquid. Vegetable water should be saved in most instances because of its mineral and vitamin content. Not only does it generally make a palatable beverage, but it is usually an excellent stock for soups and sauces and gravies.

If there's anything more soul satisfying than leaning against a log with an outdoor fire warm in front of you and plenty of first rate food secured by your own ingenuity cooking at arm's length, we've never discovered it.

We regretted only that we couldn't find any purslane with which to recreate Thoreau's experience: "I have made a satisfactory dinner simply off a dish of purslane which I gathered, boiled and salted. Yet men have come to such a pass that they frequently starve, not for want of necessaries but for want of luxuries."

The quotation reminded us that we'd purposely brought no salt. An Indian substitute, Brad volunteered, is a pinch of wood ashes, but I decided I didn't miss it that much.

When exploring the shores of the lake that afternoon, we found the scattered skeletons of two recently killed moose. Other moose were still around, for one could see their slim cattle-like prints in mud and snow, and there was the tremendous track of a grizzly, too.

"Big Siberians got these fellows," Brad said, pointing to where sun-enlarged tracks were still frozen in an area of neve packed almost as hard as a skating rink. "This, being the only lake for miles around, is a natural water hole for all sorts of game. It must be a regular slaughter house for those wolves."

We gathered some of the leg bones. I thought of how men, strayed and starving, must sometimes unwittingly curse such things when they stumble over them. Yet skeletons like these can mean salvation itself. If the animal was in good condition, the iron-rich marrow will abound in phosphorous. These humanly necessary fats are not surpassed by any food in caloric strength.

Some squaws we've met prepare a particularly invigorating dish by boiling small bones until they become gelatinous. The larger bones, however, should not be roasted into friability as some Indians we know do. Food value will be conserved if, instead, they are shattered and then simmered into nutritious broth. That is what we did now.

"Now for that browse bed," Brad promised, smacking his lips over an experimental spoonful.

"I'll help," I echoed. "Are you going to make it the same way we did that first one?"

"What first one?" he asked, puzzled.

"That one we made when we had to stay out all night up above Box Canyon," I insisted.

"Oh, that," he dismissed scornfully. "That was just a few spruce limbs we threw down in a minute or so. You thatch a real browse bed. It takes more like half an hour. We're going to need a lot of the springiest evergreen boughs we can find."

Cutting and staking four poles together in a bed-sized rectangle, Brad started the ceremony with a deep layer of small spruce branches at the head.

"They go like this," he showed me, "with the undersides up, opposite to the way they grow. The butts, which we keep well covered, point toward the foot."

Row after row was laid closely together in this manner until the mattress was about a foot thick. Then Brad made it as level and resilient as possible with soft evergreen tips shoved in wherever feasible. I helped him cover the aromatic surface with the saddle blankets, securing their edges with the poles.

"Uuuum," I enthused when I tried it. "That's comfy. It smells so wonderful, too."

"Want to top off with some spruce tea before we turn in?" he suggested.

"Is there such a thing?"

"I had to use part of young Jackie and Billy Otis's Christmas tree one year," he reminisced, "when Eleanor and Bill, their parents, thought I was joking about spruce tea. These new young tufts are a lot less strong, though."

He tossed a handful of bright emerald clusters into a suspended pot of lake water as soon as bubbles danced to its silvery surface. Then he set the concoction away from the fire to steep. Five minutes later, I cautiously sipped the result.

"Isn't it," and I hesitated, seeking the right epithet, "Christmasy!"

He nodded, grinning.

"I got all involved, trying to describe it to Jockonovitch and his folks that time, and now you peg it in just one word. It does taste the way it smells, doesn't it?" He took a swallow. "This brew can be pretty important sometimes, too."

"Important how?" I asked, interested.

"When you make it by steeping evergreen needles with an equal amount of water, it contains nearly as much Vitamin C as a similar amount of the average orange juice." He grinned again, then rimed jocosely, "A cup a day, says Doctor Gray, will surely keep scurvy away."

"Will it really?" I asked.

"It sure will," he responded. "You know how deadly a

thing scurvy can be, I guess. You remember what we've heard and read about it in the North. Why, it wasn't far from here that a one-time trapping associate of Jim Ross was found dead of scurvy. And do you know where they finally discovered his body? Leaning up against a spruce tree that, if he'd only realized it, could have saved his life!"

Scurvy, I recalled, is considered the final reason why none of the Sir John Franklin party ever got back to civilization. The explorer and 128 men had sailed from England in 1845 aboard three lavishly equipped ships in an attempt to find the Northwest Passage. Scurvy, too, killed and disabled thousands who stampeded toward the glittering Yukon River following the discovery of gold there in 1896. It made potatoes occasionally bring their weight in gold, because in raw potatoes is the mysterious Vitamin C which stops teeth from falling out, which abruptly checks certain hemorrhages and which restores vigor like a vital fire to sagging bodies.

"The ironic twist to the whole thing," Brad said, "is that there's seldom any need for anyone in the wilderness to suffer from . . . well, it's actually a vitamin-deficiency disease. Even if one depends only on purchased supplies, one ounce of cevitamic acid will prevent scurviness in one adult for a year and a half. That's Vitamin C in crystalline form. But we can get all the vitamin we want free."

Wild rose hips, which had been gay orange dots in the bush about our cabin ever since we'd built it, are also rich in the anti-scurvy constituent. I'd early formed the habit of munching these seed-filled members of the apple family when out walking. Plenty of rare fresh meat will, if all parts of the animal are used, also keep one safe from scurvy. One can live exclusively on such a diet for months and years, in fact, and keep perfectly nourished.

One need only eat all delicious portions of the animal, Brad qualified now, and not destroy valuable food elements by overcooking. The less meat and other foods are heated anyway, I noted, the greater is their food value. That went for brewing spruce tea, too, he agreed.

"What city girl ever would have dreamed such a deadly problem could be solved so simply?" I thought. I took another sip of the aromatic beverage, then added to myself with sweet relish, "And so delightfully!"

The friendly warmth of leaping flames was enhanced by the damp freshness that the corroded-copper lake imparted at dusk. Whisper-winged owls hooo-ho-ho-hooooooed through the shadows, and there was the whistle overhead of speeding ducks.

"Ready to turn in?" Brad asked, and my answer became lost in a sufficing yawn.

While we lay under our single eiderdown, as Chinook and Cloud stirred reassuringly nearby on their picket ropes, we heard wolves howling close at hand for two nights in a row with all the sweet violent yearning of the wilderness.

It was against a backdrop of such personal observations that we based our article when we returned home, three evenings later, a little lonesome for the horses. We wondered if some day soon we could afford to buy mounts like these two.

"Where shall we try this yarn?" Brad hesitated when I whirred the final rewritten page from the typewriter.

"Why not send it to one of those big hunting and fishing magazines?" I suggested. "We can always try the smaller markets later on if we have to."

We dispatched it in the next mail day, using most of our remaining stamps and not even enclosing the usual return postage. We could better afford the time of retyping it, we decided, if it should be rejected.

CHAPTER TWENTY-ONE

BACKWOODS WIFE

"While I enjoy the friendship of the seasons, nothing can make life a burden to me," Thoreau found, and so did we. "My days were not days of the week, nor were they minced into hours and fretted by the ticking of a clock. My life was become a drama of many scenes and without an end."

I found myself actually looking forward to wash days, for example. Waxwings and grosbeaks often fluttered close when Brad and I suspended pails of water over chuckling outdoor fires. We had become neighbor to the birds, not by having imprisoned one but by having caged ourselves near them.

Watchful does and carefree fawns sometimes romped on the sandy spit of river shore opposite, reassured by two hundred yards of leaping rapids, while I lounged on a stump and scrubbed. Then there was the climaxing coolness of the brook that's the final rinse.

The current felt so suddenly delicious on my heated fingers those first weeks that more than once I peeled off for a dip. I still do, but now with even less provocation since I've learned that in this climate the convenient sun is the only towel that dripping invigorated bodies require. We spent one warm afternoon, happy as kids with mudpies, damming a pool behind a miniature reef where the crystal waters already hesitated. Besides its other advantages, this made an inviting nook to which to lag sleepy-eyed early mornings while mist was still rising from the water, and we hung wash cloths and tooth brushes from convenient trees.

When I awake with the ambitious determination to spend the day house cleaning, I generally force myself to repeat Thoreau's admonition: "Every morning was a cheerful invitation to make my life of equal simplicity with Nature herself."

That usually does the trick except during stormy hours when I actually enjoy being inside a dry cabin, with the warm knowledge that everything I need or can reasonably desire is close at hand. But on days which seem expressly made for enjoying the wilderness to which we've escaped, why should I stay indoors when I might better be out exploring with Brad, or searching upriver for fossils, or panning for gold even if no more than a few specks of color ever showed, or looking for new flowers, or taking our camera and seeing if I could capture some new part of our surroundings on film?

What this all amounts to, really, is just plain wandering around the woods. It's more fun if I give myself a motive, that's all. It seems rather pointless just to hike a mile in from the river to where hills rise to the next bench of land, then turn around and tramp back again. But what if I tell myself that perhaps I'll see a wide-eyed fox and two kits where that spring oozes out of the slope? Suppose I conjecture that maybe I'll even be able to steal close enough for a photograph?

Then the scratches of rose bushes, the slaps of resinous conifer boughs, and the exertion of crawling under dead falls I can't scale appear suddenly worthwhile. As a matter of fact, I've only seen animals drinking at the spring twice. Once it was a vixen and her young.

The other time it was two moose, the sight of which always excites me no matter how often I glimpse moose. This was when the bush was green with succulent browse, incidently, but they feasted on poplar bark as they angled out of sight. A lot of people figure moose gnaw poplar bark only in deep winter when no other food is available, but now we know that isn't true. But new tracks, both large and small, are always enticingly imprinted in the tremulous black mud. So I know I'm not fooling myself too much.

There isn't much housework to do, anyway. I wash the floor every few weeks, mostly because I like to see the bright white pine smiling up at me. I sweep once or twice a day because particles of clay chinking are always falling. There's need for periodic dusting, too, partly because of the same native plaster and partly because of the yellow clouds the wind scoops from the cutbanks upriver. But it's all clean hygienic dirt, I tell myself. It is, too.

I air the eiderdown beds regularly, because they stay softer that way and because they smell so fresh afterwards. There is washing, of course. That just about ends the matter for which, truthfully, I am glad. I used to find excuses in the city for not doing housekeeping. There, aside from the sophism in my case that I wanted the house to look lived in, the difficulty was that I had so many outside interests. The same pattern holds true here, now that I think of it.

Thoreau must have enjoyed similar ideas, for he spoke glibly of declining to add a single item to the details of housekeeping.

"A lady once offered me a mat," he remarked, "but as I had no room to spare within the house, nor time to spare within or without to shake it, I declined it, preferring to wipe my feet on the sod before my door. It is best to avoid the beginnings of evil."

A nicely phrased excuse if I've ever heard one! What he

seriously meant though, as he explained later, was that he "preferred some things to others, and especially valued freedom."

"Housework was a pleasant pastime," he said, setting forth his formula which I cheerfully follow as often as possible. "When my floor was dirty, I rose early and, setting all my furniture out of doors, dashed water on the floor, sprinkled white sand on it, and then with a broom scrubbed it clean and white."

I use soap and a brush instead.

"It was pleasant to see my whole household effects out on the grass. They seemed glad to get out themselves and unwilling to be brought in. I was sometimes tempted to spread an awning over them and take my seat there. It was worthwhile to see the sun shine on these things, and hear the free wind blow on them; so much more interesting most familiar objects look out of doors than in the house.

"A bird sits on the next bough, life-everlasting grows under the table, and blackberry vines run round its legs. Pine cones, chestnut burrs, and strawberry leaves are strewn about. It looked as if this was the way these forms came to be transferred to our furniture, to tables, chairs, and bedsteads—because they once stood in their midst."

The biggest item of housekeeping anywhere, of course, revolves about cooking. There was no escape from this in the wilderness. Our appetites, as a matter of fact, proved to be a whole lot healthier and more robust in the woods.

That means I have to cook more. This does not necessarily result in additional work, I should admit. I just cook more of each dish. It's as easy to grill three pounds of steak for a dinner as one-third that amount. Potatoes can be roasting in the oven as well as not, and water for tea can be bubbling on the back of the stove. That, plus some greens and some fruit, makes a pretty good noonday meal. If we can't clean up all the steak, any remaining tidbits are especially tasty in mulligans. When we have plenty of meat, I try to cook too much rather than too little for this reason.

The bush cook, meager though her choice of materials may be, has one tremendous advantage over the most lavishly equipped city chef. The autocrat of the city kitchen too often has to stimulate the small appetites of dyspeptics. The pot and pan wielder of the wilderness has hearty appetite for an ally.

Brad is an example of what I mean. Back in the metropolis he used to be chronically troubled with what doctors, after much prodding and picturing, periodically called nervous indigestion. He was regularly put on various but similar diets. He couldn't eat this unless it was well cooked. He couldn't touch that in any form. Salads, for instance, were prohibited. Too much bulk. So was whole wheat bread. Too irritating. Tea and coffee were banned. Too stimulating. The suggestion of any more meals at the East Indian nook we had enjoyed brought shudders. Too many condiments.

"A bland diet," he was solemnly prescribed, "and not too much of that. Two crackers and a glass of milk—lukewarm, mind you, not cold—when you get hungry between times. So many drops of tincture of belladonna in so much water as usual a half hour before each meal, of course, and let's try these pills which just came out."

That must have been one underlying reason he was so anxious to go to the wilderness. On the fishing and hunting trips he regularly took on the Southwest Miramichi River in New Brunswick, the Grand Cascapedia River in Quebec, and throughout northern New England he always felt fine. There was nothing organically wrong, physicians said, and one of them added a sombre "yet." It was the tense, artificial haste and worry of city life, and many of our acquaintances suffered with similar complaints. A surprising number of them had ulcers, the occupational disease of the theatrical and writing professions.

"Making yourselves sick," accurately diagnosed Thoreau, "that you may lay up something against a sick day!"

The nervous indigestion vanished once we moved into a log cabin. It disappeared in spite of my cooking, too, and that's saying a lot.

A big advantage I had in my wilderness kitchen was that I wasn't already a skilled city cook. There is a tremendous gap between the sort of culinary artistry embracing electrical gadgets and delicately contrived automatic ovens on one hand and, on the other, a wood stove, I can understand why some really good cooks, despairing early, never span it. I had no so-conditioned reflexes to unblock.

Water boiled over crackling sweet-scented poplar, too, except that it took longer. Cheese sandwiches melted and bubbled deliciously in the oven of a wood stove, also. Except for being able to draw a few such parallels, I started in practically from scratch. As I was already coming to realize, I was lucky.

Anyone informing an experienced cook as Dudley had me that two tablespoons of fresh light snow will take the place of each egg in a batter would have been put in his place in no uncertain fashion. But I didn't know enough not to try it. It worked.

What culinary artist wouldn't have turned up an disbelieving nose when advised by Jessie and Dennis Murphy that the white of wood ashes, used part for part, is a satisfactory kitchen substitute for baking soda? I just took it as a matter of course when everything came out all right.

One does wonderful things in this wilderness with such a common commodity as wood ashes. Dudley showed me how he can roll his beautifully kneaded dough in flour and bury it in hot ashes. When a straw thrust through the middle comes out clean and dry, the biscuits are done—and delicious. You can do this with ordinary bread and biscuits. Or you can bake ash cakes which, Brad proved to me, any trail cook can prepare at ax-stroke speed by mixing two cups of corn meal and a half-teaspoon of salt with enough lukewarm water to make a stiff batter.

Even when the meal is over, the wilderness wife finds herself still reveling in ashes. Greasy pans practically clean themselves when water and wood ashes are boiled in them. The lye turns the grease to soap, I discovered. You can also dip a freshly cut potato in ashes and use it to polish rusty silverware. Vesta Gething showed me that quirk.

"High-bush cranberries make better applesauce than prunes," someone remarked one day down at the Hudson's Bay Company, and that gave me an idea.

I started work on an article that might interest one of the women's magazines, I hoped, describing the wonderful lot of the backwoods wife who if she hasn't got what she'd ordinarily need, just substitutes something else. We were still waiting for a reaction to the wild foods piece.

When I came to telling about sourdough bread, I felt so suddenly incompetent that I decided to try another batch. Perhaps what happened resulted from the stimulus imparted by Dudley's fourteen year old sourdough. Or maybe it was because I was just too plain disgusted because of other failures to spend much time on this latest experiment. Anyway, I slammed the dough into shape, thumped it into pans, and without a whole lot of fussing shoved these into the oven when a glance decided me they'd risen as much as they were going to rise. I didn't keep peeking in and letting out heat, either.

They came out so wonderfully fat and brown that I just sat down and stared. The trouble, I finally decided, was that in being cautious and painstaking I must have somehow allowed too much of the leavening gas to escape. But would the same procedure work again? It did. I tried it with yeast instead of sourdough. The result was still real bread. So the knack was as simple as all that!

Dudley had by this time acquired the habit of bringing his own bread when he came to lunch. He unblinkingly asserted that it was only "to even things up." I noticed that afterwards Dudley evened things up in other ways.

My supreme moment came the June afternoon he disappeared down the aisle in the forest with one of my loaves bulging in his pack.

CHAPTER TWENTY-TWO

DAY AT MIDNIGHT

"I spaded up all the land which I required for my beans, potatoes, corn, peas, and turnips. I learned that if one would live simply and eat only the crop he raised, and raise no more than he ate, he would need to cultivate only a few rods of ground. He could do all his necessary farm work as it were with his left hand at odd hours in the summer.

"It is not necessary," Thoreau adjured, "that a man should earn his living by the sweat of his brow, unless he sweats easier than I do."

Vegetables in the tiny garden we dug with our folding shovel in a single morning grew to amazing proportions during sunny days so prolonged that now, in June, we were able to read outdoors at midnight. The seed advertisements of Eaton's and Simpson's, Canada's two large mail order houses, had been so alluring that it was only with the utmost of restrain that we confined ourselves to radishes, carrots, turnips, cabbage, lettuce, onions and potatoes.

Trapper, prospector, homesteader, everybody had his own garden. I, at least, had thought vaguely of the North as being cold and unproductive. The speed with which seeds put on their green Spring bonnets while daylight worked on twenty-hour shifts . . . well, it was amazing.

"Frightful jungle around my cabin," Dudley described with no more than his usual amount of understatement. "Had to chop a path through the rhubarb yesterday to reach my front door. Ghastly."

Growth did become almost tropical in its intensity. Heavily leafing bush now cozily framed the cabin. Only along the broad sweep of the river did we now have an unimpeded view. White blossoms that whispered of juicy wild strawberries hid like forgotten snowflakes close to the sheltering ground. Other flowers promised blueberries, saskatoons, thimbleberries, raspberries, wild cherries, and two species of cranberries. As we awaited these new wild crops, we stuffed ourselves joyously with fresh greens in a vain effort to keep abreast of the present supply.

"Every time I think of those spring canoe trips I used to take I could kick myself," Brad said. "We became so starved for greens that the first thing we did when getting Outside was order huge salads. Just think of the fiddleheads and other delicacies we passed up."

The fly season proved here to hold no threats. Tiny pestiferous mosquitoes had appeared suddenly on the first day of June, but they were not at all bothersome near the river. When we went back into the bush, we daubed on the colorless and rather pleasant fly dope which, Brad was forced to admit, keeps insects away far better than the old-fashioned pine-tar preparations to which he'd become accustomed. Blue, we found, was the mosquitoes' favorite color. They preferred damp clothing to dry.

There were none of the little black flies Brad had been dreading. No-see-ums, microscopic winged drillers, swooped down briefly at dusk and again when the twilight deepened into dawn, but all one had to do was rub on a palmful of the repellent or wait indoors a short while.

"Why," I decided, surprised after all the stories I'd been hearing of night-long smudges and suffocating mosquito nets, "the fly season here isn't even as bad as it is on Cape Cod."

Mornings, a hurried sleepy struggle during our city captivity, had weeks before been transformed into beckoning invitations that lured us early from our eiderdowns most days, eager to share whatever nature had to offer. We ate our breakfasts now, when yellow wolf-willow enchanted the breeze with incredibly sweet perfume, on the often successful look for moose, deer, bear, and other animals drinking from the river.

Considering the probable reaction of some of my city acquaintances as I drew specific parallels between my and Thoreau's days, I had to agree: "This was sheer idleness to my fellow townsmen, no doubt. But if the birds and flowers had tried me by their standard, I should not have been found wanting."

Brad and I found ourselves wondering, more and more often these serene June days, how did two city people happen to be living the way so many millions only dream about? It's true that we had determined almost from childhood to escape from man-made artificialities to the unimproved works of God.

But doubtless others have also long planned to take to the woods—plan still and do nothing about it. One of these days they're going to have "enough time" and "enough money." Then the chroniclers of frontiersmen like Mr. Daniel Boone and Mr. Christopher Carson had better take notice.

Yet there they are, and here are we—in a log cabin that lazes near the edge of a clay-ironstone precipice where cliff swallows swoop brilliantly to suspended colonies of gourd-like nests. A mountain brook, gently now, sparkles past our door before hurling itself in a diamond torrent to the primeval river a hundred feet below. I wished we actually owned this land, although for all practical purposes we really were monarchs of all we surveyed.

Down river to the east were the smokes of the closest settlement where, six miles along an always interesting trail, several dozen log cabins cluster restfully about a red-roofed HB.C. trading post. Slopes, fragrant with lodgepole pine and blue spruce, cup this expanse in sheltered solitude.

There was only one discordant note. If something didn't happen soon, we were going to be without store supplies and without money.

Mail day came around again. I was in the midst of coloring some cloth a nice fresh yellow with alder bark and setting the hue with a nickel's worth of iron sulphate. I planned to make cushions sometime later. The process had taken longer than I'd expected, and now I couldn't leave. I wasn't even sure I wanted to go to the Hope. If we were going to have this happiness only a little longer, I wanted to enjoy every moment possible in our log home. Brad put on his packsack to carry back a bundle of library books and some magazines we'd borrowed from the Pecks and the Ohlands.

"Here, sweet," Brad said. He pressed a wad of paper unexpectedly into my hand. With a man's idea of a good-by kiss, he was out of the door. "Keep your fingers crossed."

As he swung down the trail, I realized how much vigor and enthusiasm this log cabin life had returned to him. I didn't want to be forced back to the city.

"The mass of men lead lives of quiet desperation." Our discussion that afternoon we'd decided to leave for the wilderness became vivid in my mind. "The incessant anxiety and strain is a well-nigh incurable form of disease. One has no time to be anything but a machine. It is a fool's life. I am convinced from experience that to maintain one's self on this earth is not a hardship but a pastime, if we will live simply and wisely."

One reaction crowding the heels of war, as it has all wars, is a yearning to return to the land. Modern pioneers of both sexes, who would have stayed passively cramped in cities if not jolted from their ruts by battle, want to laugh in farther places . . . where wild foods are free for the gathering, fuel for the cutting, and habitation for the satisfaction of building.

The reversion toward the simple life, I decided, is as wholesome as eggs and cream. Not everybody realizes that fifty years ago less than four of every 100 Americans lived in communities of 8000 or more. But at the start of the Second World War, over half the country's population was so confined.

Scientists remind us that nature intended human beings should spend most of their hours beneath open skies. With appetites sharpened by robust living, they should eat plain food. They should live at self regulated paces, unoppressed by artificial hurry and worry of man-mismade civilization. I sighed. To any who would join this procession back to the soil, I thought, what from my brief experience could I say? Only, I decided, that our single regret was that we'd put it off so long!

"Search the scarlet spiral," I read when I opened the note Brad had left with me.

We'd played the game before. I entered into it now, between sessions with kettle and dye, to keep my thoughts from twisting into desolate, maddening tangles. A message tucked into a spool of red thread, when I thought to look there, directed me to a second hiding place.

Clew followed clew. The hunt became so engrossing that between it and the wild dye, I forgot lunch. At last, I fondled the exciting pliable package that Brad had secreted among the firewood.

He'd wrapped it painstakingly in layers of birch bark. Eagerly, I untied dozens of teasing knots. It was one of our rules that none should be cut, and eons seemed to drag by. I smelled the smoke-sweet loveliness of moosehide before I uncovered the pair of high native moccasins. Eyes wet, I realized they were just what I needed to follow silently the now dry forest trails.

"If everything works out for us soon enough, you'll be needing these," the enclosed message said, and I tried to look away until the sob left my breathing, but my eyes kept straying back.

"No matter what, Vena, I love you. You were right. In a city, husbands and wives can't possibly realize how much they may need one another. I've loved you more and more these months in the wilderness, although *more* never seemed possible."

The afternoon dragged by slowly. I thought that hours might turn into minutes if I busied myself, so I started a mulligan. I commenced by frying with some beaver lard in the bottom of our largest pot a sliced chunk of bear meat that had been soaking overnight in water to de-spice it sufficiently for use in cooking.

The Hornaday process was working out excellently for us. Brushed free of excess spice and thinly sliced, the greatly shrunken cured meat reminded us of particularly tasty commercial dried beef. We liked to munch it while on the trail.

Now, I added to the sizzling meat a cupful of chopped onions, stirring so that everything would brown well. In went two tablespoons of sugar to improve the flavor. Then I mixed in enough flour to make a thick body.

Boiling water followed, and I slid the covered pot onto the back of the stove to simmer for the remainder of the day. Potatoes, turnips, and carrots I cleaned so that they could be sliced into the stew shortly before I thought Brad would return.

Then I forked together in bannock proportions two cups of flour, two teaspoons of baking powder, and a half-teaspoon of salt. Ten minutes before we ate, I planned to add enough milk to make a soft dough. This I meant to spoon in globs atop the mulligan where they'd cook into dumplings. As a matter of fact. I forgot all about dumplings.

Blue shadows along the more sheltered portions of the river deepened to amethysts and purples. Coyotes started to ki-yi up above Box Canyon. When I heard feet outside, I scrambled to light the lamp although the cabin was not really dark. It took four matches. Then the latch rattled and door creaked. A heavy pack clumped on the floor.

"Phew," Brad said. "That was heavy."

"What have you got?"

"Groceries." Then he saw my look and grinned. "Yep, I charged them at the Bay, but don't worry."

"The stories came back?"

In answer, he reached into an outer pocket of the pack. Two long heavy envelopes slapped on the table. I watched him take out another envelope. It was long, too, but it did not seem bulky. A tiny bit of colored paper protruded beyond the flap. It was a check for eighty dollars.

"Your hunch was right," Brad chuckled. "That outdoor magazine snapped up our article on wild foods. Maybe that's the answer. No more fiction. We'll just write about facts we know. Darling, say something. . . . Don't you realize what this means, darling? Honey, we'll never have to leave our wilderness home unless we want."

For some reason, I was thinking once more of the millions of other city couples who must be dreaming of a similar escape to God's unspoiled spaces; dreaming and letting it go at that.

"'If one advances confidently in the direction of his dreams, and endeavors to live the life which he has imagined, he will meet with a success unexpected in common hours.'" My arms tightened about Brad, as still another fear disappeared. "Oh, darling, darling. Yes, dreams do come true."

CHAPTER TWENTY-THREE

PERIL IN THE PINES

They used to get after Thoreau, too, about the dangers of living in the woods. He had some pretty good answers, including the famous: "Nothing is so much to be feared as fear."

Another of Thoreau's replies that we like was, "A man sits as many risks as he runs." This seems to describe his and our situation extremely well.

"The old and infirm and the timid, of whatever age or sex, thought most of sickness and sudden accident and death," Thoreau said, all of which indicates that human nature hasn't changed much during the past one hundred years.

"To them life seemed full of danger. They thought that a prudent man would carefully select the safest position, where Dr. B. might be on hand at a moment's warning. To them the village was a league for mutual defense. You would suppose that they would not go a-huckleberrying without a medicine chest. The amount of it is, if a man is alive, there is always danger that he may die, though the danger must be allowed to be less in proportion as he is dead-and-alive to begin with."

How far away is the nearest doctor, some asked us when

we first spoke of living in northern British Columbia? At what distance is the closest hospital? When we replied that the answer to both questions is Fort St. John, about sixty-five miles away over what might be described most charitably as an unpaved road, consternation was acute.

I even began to feel doubtful until I told myself that if our ancestors had felt that way, they'd still be huddling along the Eastern seaboard if they had dared venture into this New World at all. Then I started to draw other hypothetical situations, the outcome of which was the conclusion that, everything considered, Brad and I actually would be a whole lot safer in the wilderness than in a city.

Both of us had been so healthy since our arrival, as a matter of fact, that we'd had no excuse to visit any of the excellent doctors in either Fort St. John or Dawson Creek. One of them we've particularly desired to meet, too, ever since hearing how he kept a rubber sponge attached protectively to his car's roof above the driver's seat and how in his gas tank was ingeniously suspended a cowbell which clanged a warning when the fuel level became too low to deaden it.

Medical surveys confirm that colds are far more rare among the white population of the North, for all its spectacular climate, than in the comparatively healthy and medicine-conscious United States. Carefully documented military records, too, support the revealing assertion that the armed services have encountered almost no health problems in the arctic and subarctic.

We'd had one cold apiece since our arrival. That was after a cheechako did some sneezing after hiking upriver for a view of Rocky Mountain Canyon, which in the manner of tenderfeet he'd been unawaredly paralleling all the way from Hudson Hope. You don't get cold from wandering about in the wet woods all day, or from sitting in a draft, or from letting wet boots dry on your feet, or from standing outside in pajamas or less on a sub-zero night for a glimpse of some particularly startling celestial fireworks. We did all these things without any apparent ill effects.

One more fear disappeared when that check arrived for our successful account of wild foods. If we could make one sale, we assured ourselves, we could make others. Besides, we knew money would be a problem anywhere, and here at least we didn't require much of it. We both started other factual articles, I for the juvenile markets that so far had remained aloof from all my attempts at fiction.

What else was there to fear? Accidents? They are, of course, a constant threat in the wilderness as well as anywhere else. The main danger is that if you get hurt while back of beyond, you may really be in a predicament. The fact that everyone realizes subconsciously that what may be only a minor mischance in the city can turn out to be fatal when there's no one nearby to help is, I believe, the major reason why there aren't more mishaps in the wilderness. Anyone who lives for long in the farther places gets the habit of being careful.

Then, too, folks who spend very much time in unmapped regions become self reliant. When Don Peck's horse fell with him in such a way that Don was left stranded in the bush with a dislocated hip, he tied his foot to one tree and hauled on a second until the bone snapped back into the socket.

When Dick Hamilton was temporarily blinded by a snapping fragment of metal in his trapping cabin, so far back in the mountains that there was no chance of getting help before Spring, he at once rigged guide lines between the door and such vital spots as the creek and the wood pile. When help did come by months later, the infection had long since dimmed the other eye, but Dick was in shape to travel. Friends got him out to Prince George where an operation restored perfect vision. These are pretty drastic examples, but they show what can happen.

We came—Dr. Thomas J. Gray tells us—equipped for taking care of misadventures. We didn't arrive loaded down, in other words, with a lot of things we'd probably never need and wouldn't know how to use if we should. We brought a few assorted bandages, compresses, gauze, adhesive tape, several packets of small adhesive bandages particularly handy for small cuts and blisters, tincture of iodine for which we later substituted tincture of metaphen, some rubbing alcohol, a thermometer, tannic acid jelly for burns, an aspirin compound, several ampules of morphine just in case, and a long strip of innertube for possible use as a tourniquet.

We have arnica because we make it ourselves, soaking the bright yellow blossoms in alcohol. We occasionally daub this on a bruise for the same reason. That just about completes our medicine chest except for a mentholated salve we use for chapped lips. Brad brought along a supply of tincture of belladonna which, unused in the absence of nervous indigestion, has pretty well dried to a greenish blur by now. And that's that.

Plain ordinary table salt, a rounded teaspoon in a quart of warm water taken preferably on an empty stomach, serves as a purge whenever someone happens by who wants a laxative. Living this sort of life, we don't. A teaspoon of salt in a glass of water is medically regarded as equal to commercial mouth washes. Baking soda, incidently, is as good a dentifrice as most and far less expensive than any of the manufactured brands.

What about forest fires? They're destructive here but not dangerous. A few white settlers and a lot of Indians set them regularly to clear land for cattle grazing and for hunting, and no one takes any action against them. The fires mostly burn slowly and deliberately, crowning only occasionally. During winter a lot of them smoulder deep in the peat-like vegetable matter of muskegs, bursting into flame again when snow leaves the land.

They've never killed nor even seriously injured anyone

here, and they've certainly never forced anyone to take to
water for protection. It seems too bad that they're so savagely magnificent and that they actually do provide better
grazing and better hunting for at least a few years. They
leave such ugly, twisted wastes.

What about that carefully phrased query, voiced by the
Back Bay maiden lady who stanchly put aside the Sunday
comic sheets each week not to be perused until Monday?
What if an Indian should chance to pass while I was swimming alone, and presumedly ungarbed, in some wilderness
water? Well, he'd either retire from that vicinity so quickly
and softly that I'd never sense his presence, or he'd continue
along without delay in the pretense that he was totally un-
aware of me.

The implications of the thus posed problem went deeper,
of course. The whole answer is that a woman is historically
a great deal safer from either minor annoyance or major vio-
lence in the wilderness than when strolling, alone or es-
corted, along the lovely Esplanade in Boston, or through
New York's enjoyable Central Park, or in any other heavily
frequented and accordingly well patrolled city rusticity. No
woman we or any of our friends have ever known about has
ever been molested in any way whatsoever in or around
Hudson Hope, and that is that.

What about wild beasts? The truth is that the most dangerous animals here, as elsewhere on this continent, are the
plain barnyard variety of bulls. No one at Hudson Hope has
ever been hurt by a wolf, grizzly, black bear, mountain lion,
or any other wild animal.

Joe Turner, however, was killed in his own yard by his
bull. Leo Rutledge, an outfitter for big game hunts, has never
been threatened by any wild animal, but a domestic bull
kept him on an uncomfortable perch for hours. Other local
inhabitants have been harassed by bulls who, incidently,
are color blind and therefore don't need to see any particular

hue to become provoked. Larry Gething, Dennis Murphy, Joe Barkley, Charlie Ohland, Bobby Beattie, Hughie Murray, Gary Powell, Mel Kyllo, Matt Boe, and everyone else here who has spent much time around bulls agrees he's a lot more wary of them than of anything wandering wild in the bush.

A bugaboo that terrifies a lot of city folks in the woods is a fear of becoming lost. We realize that being lost can be a very serious matter, especially in largely unmapped and unexplored wilderness such as this. On the hand, there's not the slightest reason for either of us to get lost.

Oh, I don't mean that we may not have to stay out overnight sometimes. That can happen to anyone. Making camp before darkness settles down is a whole lot more sensible than blundering very far through the bush and taking a chance, for instance, of getting poked in the eye by a dead branch.

But we'd have to work at it even under extreme conditions to become really lost. The Peace River, you see, flows generally from west to east past here. Our cabin is on the sunny north bank. That means that any time we keep heading south while on this side, we're bound to reach the river. If we're across the Peace, we merely have to reverse the process and strike north. Then it's only a matter of following the stream. The country varies enough, becoming increasingly mountainous west of the cabin and flattening to eventual plains east of it, so that even when land marks are hidden we're not apt to follow in the wrong direction very far.

Dread of starving is probably the foremost terror of anyone caught in the wilderness. Starvation is no fun. The body begins living on its own flesh after a few foodless hours. The carbohydrates go first, followed by the fats. Then proteins from sinews and muscles keep the human machine functioning.

But the fact is that nearly every part of this continent

abounds with wild edibles. We sometimes find ourselves living almost entirely off the country for days at a time. Of course, we just take the pick of things. No possible sustenance should be overlooked if one is actually in need.

Shell piles beside a stream may be the clue to a mussel bed. The buzzing of bees about a hollow tree often indicates that a smoky fire may be in order. Frog legs are nourishing. So is snake meat. Even the riper bird eggs should not be scorned.

When anyone speaks of living off the country, the city listener in particular starts thinking of venison steaks and moose saddles. The trouble is that even here, in what is an unspoiled a wilderness as can be found anywhere, Indians and sourdoughs occasionally hunt fruitlessly for weeks without even seeing big game. One just can't depend on getting large animals when he needs them. Edible berries, nuts, barks, leaves, stalks, and roots should therefore be the working basis of emergency sustenance in the silent places. It seems a good idea for anyone who's going into the woods to learn to identify a few such local staples.

Groundnuts helped the Pilgrims through their first hard wintor. Thoreau upon trying them declared, "This tuber seemed like a faint promise of Nature to rear her own children and feed them simply here at some future period."

None of the millions of campers, hunters, fishermen, hikers, and just plain happy vacationists who take to the woods for awhile each year ever consciously expect to become lost, I suppose. Yet thousands do go astray every year. Numerous others are stranded by accidents. We've come to believe, from what experience we've had, that the woodland visitor not reasonably prepared for such an eventuality is in the class of those well meaning individuals who didn't know the gun was loaded.

The porcupine, like the burdock and thistle, is better fare than one might expect. The law, for one reason alone, guards.

this mobile pincushion in many localities. Why? The lethargic porky, with its chattering yellow teeth and its high weak grunt which always reminds me of what I suppose an effeminate bull moose might sound like, is the one animal which even the greenest tenderfoot can kill with a stick.

The way to prepare a porcupine, Brad and I have found, is by making an incision along the smooth belly. The skin can then be slipped off like a glove. Some animals such as wolves learned to make a harmless meal of the waddling rodent by attacking it in this unprotected area. Simpler than skinning, of course, is to toss the carcass Indian fashion into the fire. The quills will burn while the meat is roasting. But so will the fat!

"What of it?" I've heard a cheechako ask.

Sourdoughs know the answer. They'll remember northerners who have died of what is known as "rabbit starvation." It may sound incredible that a man with all the varying hares he can eat can still die because of a lack of food. It's true, nevertheless. An exclusive diet of such lean meat will cause diarrhea within several days to a week, followed by death.

The secret is to add some fat to the lean. This will forestall the protein poisoning. Accounts are common, nevertheless, of lost men who burn priceless fat—in frying, roasting, and other forms of high-temperature cookery—in order to give the nutritively inferior lean meat a "better flavor."

When starvation threatens, nothing should be cooked longer than is necessary for palatableness except when there are germs to be destroyed. Vegetables are generally more nutritive raw. Even the practice of toasting bread decreases both nourishment and digestibility. The less meat is cooked, the greater is its food value.

Another fatal mistake the lost man may make is to concentrate too much time and energy in fishing. Royal Canadian Mounted Police scientists assert that such fresh-water fish as perch, bass, pickerel, and pike average only some 200 calories per live pound. A man living an active outdoor life requires upwards of 4500 calories daily.

Practices ordinarily contrary to good sportsmanship become warrantable when one is lost and starving. Who can say that jigging with an unraveled thread and sharpened crotched stick isn't then justified if it will produce food? Even dry-fly purists will admit cornering trout and killing them with clubs when necessity has demanded. Fast rocky streams offer many an easy mess if one will wade along carefully and feel under the up-current sides of stones. Such natural traps imprison numerous piscatory prizes.

Certain Indian methods of fishing may prove lifesavers for the hungry wayfarer. One procedure is to crush the leaves and stalk of the mullein or fish weed (*croton setigerus*). These are then dropped into a still pool or temporarily dammed brook. The fish therein, momentarily narcotized, will float to the surface where they should be immediately secured.

The bulbous root of the so-called soap plant (*chlorogalum pomdeidianum*) can be similarly used. So can the seeds of the southern buckeye (*aesculus pavia*). Fish caught by these emergency means are as wholesome as if merely dazed by concussion.

Ptarmigan, grouse, partridge, and other such game birds promise feasts for those astray in the Silent Places. A stick, stone, or knot of wood is many times the only weapon needed. If one misses with the first throw, the fowl will often give a second and third chance. Sometimes they'll even allow one to knock them off a branch with a long limb.

The alert wanderer will sometimes scare an owl from a fresh kill and a potential supper for himself. Fox, coyotes, and wolves are also occasionally surprised at fresh meals. These predators almost invariably melt into the bush at the approach of a human being.

But if one comes upon a bear at its kill, it is wise to look around for a tree or exit unless one is armed and experienced. The bear, particularly if it is a black, probably won't offer any argument. Yet it may. If you're weaponless and still need that meat enough to warrant the risk, you can watch your chance and build a fire beside it. You should have plenty of fuel at hand, especially if night is near. And watch out. Grizzlies, for one, have a habit of dropping down close to their food.

Nearly every part of North American game is edible. A possible exception is polar bear liver which may be poisonous to some degree at certain times. Even gall has uses as seasoning. Some local old-timers have also informed Brad that they save the gall sacs of bears, puncture them, let out the gall, dry the sac, powder it, and then eat it for potency.

Blood certainly should not be wasted. Two ounces daily fulfill human iron requirements. It would take ten eggs to accomplish the same thing. Vital organs, too often discarded, abound with indispensable minerals and vitamins. Up here, where we ordinarily have all the muscle meat we can use, we have come to regard them as particularly delicious tidbits.

Hides are as nourishing as lean meat. This means that tossing a hide into a fire, as many do to burn off the hair, results in a considerable amount of nutriment going up in smoke.

Eskimos depend on the salad-like contents of caribou stomachs for greens. Some Indian tribes, too, feast on the vegetable contents of herbivorous animals. A thrifty aboriginal way of preparing birds and small animals for the pot, as a matter of fact, is beating them to a pulp, entrails and all.

Taste habits become relatively unimportant when one is warding off starvation. That is why it may be profitable to remember that some Indians use rabbit excrement to thicken wild vegetable soup. Others drape unemptied deer intestines on roasting racks. Well, don't many so-called refined city folk relish raw oysters, odiferous cheese, and whole sardines?

"It's true," Brad says, "that under favorable conditions the human body can fend off starvation for one or two months by living off its own tissues. But why be a cannibal?"

CHAPTER TWENTY-FOUR

A RIVER CRUISE

Days became shorter and crisper. When we were awakened by a metallic thundering one September morning shortly before eight o'clock, darkness was still a deep translucent blue.

The racket was startling. Seeing Brad leap to the floor, I squirmed with almost frantic haste from the suddenly confining softness of my eiderdown. The door creaked slightly on its old hinges. The noise was lost in a fresh burst of sound, so close that it seemed loud enough to drown out anything short of an explosion. Spruce needles, slippery with dew, moved beneath my moccasins.

Brad lowered the rifle he had grabbed. I saw him grin. Reaching his side and looking upward in the plane that the tilt of his head indicated, I couldn't control a smile. Clinging to the rust-streaked rim of our stovepipe was a small, brightly colored bird.

"A doggone woodpecker," Brad whispered. "It must be mixed up in its seasons. They generally do that sort of hammering in the Spring. Listen, Vena."

I could hear a faint tat-a-tat-ta-tat-tat sounding from deep in the forest. The woodpecker on our stovepipe cocked its head. It poised a beak and waited with showmanship for the noise to subside. Then it rolled off another dramatic response on the rusty metal.

"Isn't that the doggone smartest woodpecker you ever saw?" Brad demanded, half disgruntled and half admiring. "Isn't that a Thomas A. Edison of woodpeckers, improving on old fashioned methods with sleep no object? The other one we hear is pecking on a dead tree. That sound doesn't carry too far. Our side-kick here has discovered it can get better coverage by going to work on our stovepipe. It really believes in advertising, doesn't it?"

The woodpecker sitting up there on the smoke vent cocked its head, as if proud to see enterprise recognized. Then it winged away in a flash of color. Taking a stick, I beat on a dead stump in similar cadence. The unseen bird replied. Then Brad tried it, and the answer came once more.

"Let's go and wash up before one of them gets jealous," I suggested finally, glancing up at the dimming stars and thinking how, with so much electricity, one never really sees them in cities. "With the days getting shorter this way, we're sleeping later and later. I'd like some coffee. How about you?"

"And some *tiger* and eggs," he echoed, "Dudley's brand of tiger, that is. Say, look at that."

A fringe of ice lay, still and prophetic, along both shores of our bathing pool. It tinkled like crystal when we broke through to wash.

" 'I did not plaster till it was freezing weather,' " Brad read portentously from our old copy of Thoreau's *Walden* when we returned to the cabin. "You and I had better take care of our yearly chinking right now before the weather gets really cold. We could finish it before noon if we get an early start. Do you have anything scheduled for today?"

"Nothing that I can't do just as well tomorrow or the day after." I shook my head. "But what are we going to use for plaster? Thoreau had lime, didn't he?"

"We," Brad expostulated, "have the sediments of the Early Cretaceous Sea, deposited before the comparatively new Rocky Mountains thrust upwards here from 3000 to 6000 feet above sea level."

"Is that," I asked, getting out the bacon, "your simple way of explaining we don't need lime?"

"There is a big lime deposit down at Dudley's," he said, "not to mention that kiln Earl Pollan and his dad, Jack, have just below the big spring at Hudson Hope."

"Oh, I'd forgotten the kiln."

"The clay we have right here will do fine," he said.

He touched a burning match to the fuzz sticks he'd set in the stove. They sprang into flame with a crackling that transferred itself hungrily to the kindling he crisscrossed in place. Smoke gusted briefly before the windows, a gossamer scarf against the pallid shoulders of dawn.

"When the villagers were lighting their fires beyond the horizon," as Thoreau had remarked, "I too gave notice to the various wild inhabitants, by a smoky streamer from my chimney, that I was awake."

After breakfast, we mixed small batches of clay and water in a pail to the consistency of thick mud. Brad slapped this in handfuls between the logs after I'd knifed out any old chinking that was loose. I pressed and smoothed the soft clay into place with the spud, the chisel-like piece of wood Brad had whittled that past winter from seasoned birch. We cleaned the logs finally with damp rags. The cabin was neatly and inexpensively insulated for another year. The sun which had finally soared above the opposite ridge at 9:25 was now clear and hot.

"I wish the water in the brook wasn't so low," I said, shoving a strand of hair out of my eyes with the back of a grimy hand. "I feel like taking a good dip before dinner."

"Let's go down to the river," Brad suggested. "The water's

so low there, too, that it makes a pretty good pool in front of the big reef just below here. Besides it's warmer there. Maybe we can catch some trout for dinner. Say, I'd better take the camera, too. Who'd think that this far North we'd be swimming in September."

Sunlight beat on the reef which now was bare all the way to the opposite shore except for a single rift, about twenty feet wide, through which a green torrent poured. I adjusted my sun glasses. The great rippled ledge, hot beneath our feet, was interesting with fossils and with coal-like fragments of petrified wood. Brad took my picture, then berated himself because it finished the roll and he'd neglected to bring a reload.

We caught in quick succession two big cutthroat trout. Deeply red beneath their lower jaws, they weighed at least four pounds apiece. Our next meal arranged for, we dived and frolicked from the reef near where our waterfall spattered on the rock in icy drops that formed their own pellucid rivulet which trickled into the Peace.

" 'I love a broad margin to my life,' " I quoted happily.

A check came later in September for my article about housekeeping in the north woods. Oddly enough, a smaller check arrived in the same mail for a reprint of the same piece. The latter I tucked carefully in a breast pocket. I had a special use for it.

The Cuthills introduced us that mail day to a doctor of anthropology from one of the big American museums. He was at Hudson Hope, preparing to cruise upriver to investigate the possibility that the original Americans, perhaps having crossed from Asia via the Bering Straits, may have followed meat animals southward and then strayed inland by way of the natural depression the Peace River made through the Rocky Mountains.

"Why don't you come along?" he invited us. "A Mr.

Boynton is going to drive us across the portage by wagon. There'll be plenty of room in that forty-foot river boat King Gething told me he's taking from there."

"It's the best time of the year to travel up the Peace," Dave encouraged, and Marion echoed, "That's the one trip in this country I've always wanted to make."

"Plenty of room," the anthropologist repeated. "There's a cave on Mt. Selwyn I want to take a look at, although the Gethings are of the opinion it's a fairly modern gravity cave. If aborigines did pass through here as I suspect, they probably lived awhile in caves."

"Oh, we couldn't get away, thanks," Dave told him. "As I told you this morning, we'd come like a shot if I could get away. You and Vena certainly shouldn't miss it, Brad."

"I'm right in the middle of a yarn," Brad hesitated, "and there's the wood pile to build up for cold weather."

"It'd be good story material," I suggested.

"The cache needs tightening up, too, before we store our winter's grubstake there," he noted, then looked at me as if anxious to be overruled.

Accordingly, I rustled the two checks.

"Haven't we something to celebrate?" I asked.

"Say, that's right," Brad echoed. "You're leaving tomorrow, Doctor? I'd better hike back now and pick up our eiderdowns and a few things."

We journied westward through the sheer backbone of the Canadian Rockies in a narrow wooden river boat propelled by an outboard motor. King Gething, occasionally shoving a brown pipe into his mouth and then as abruptly hooking it out again, steered so certainly that he scarcely seemed to glance at throw-offs and riffles.

"Look at the way he uses every inch of slack water," Brad marveled privately to me. "He knows the channel sure, but this takes an instinct, too. No wonder they call the guy the King of the River."

Except for scattered clumps of duffle bags and tarpaulin-covered boxes, the craft with only four of us aboard seemed practically empty. We moved around at will. It was an odd sensation to be boating so serenely, along an often lake-like river, through the most savagely magnificent mountains I had ever seen. The Alps, although higher, seemed domesticated to me now compared to the wild fierce grandeur of these unmapped fastnesses. There was a splendid, exalted incredibility about the scene that seemed to extend back and back, unspoiled, to the days when this part of the world was moulded.

"Yes, there's only two rapids," King Gething was saying, and his voice although soft lay distinct against the roar of the motor. "We'll run them both without any trouble, Doc. If it weren't for Rocky Mountain Canyon between the portage and Hudson Hope, we could pretty well float more than 2000 miles from the headwaters of the Finlay River to the Arctic Ocean."

My hair was whipped by a fresh breeze, alive with clean damp smell of the river and the dissimilar odors of conifers and poplars. Waves slapped against the planking of the boat. There was already an autumnal crispness in the air. As the sun swung closer toward the mountains, I could see swirling close to the water mist that would thicken into heavy white ribbons during the night.

"There's Mrs. Johnson's ranch." King Gething spoke from time to time, as we cleaved easily against the current. "There's Twelve Mile where Tommy Stott used to live. You could cross those mountains back there and drop down to Chinaman Lake. . . . Jim Beattie developed this twenty Mile flat. Jim told me his Dad said that success meant using the forces about you, and Jim was plenty successful. Finest wife and youngsters you could hope to meet."

We passed Jack Adam's old cabin at Goldbar, too, and Brennan's Flats where a lot of folks we knew had sluiced for gold. Carbon Creek gushed from the green forest a few miles farther along, and then around a bend Bob Yeomans waved from his trapping cabin by Schooler Creek. Water fowl zoomed occasionally from the liquid silver ahead. Trout slapped lazy tails.

"Here's Teepee Rocks," King announced finally, a short time after we'd heard the threatening rush of water against unseen reefs in the deepening shadows to port. He swung toward starboard. "Do you want to watch up front with a pole, Brad? We'll camp here."

Driftwood gave itself to flame with a rising, noisy eagerness. King, securing the boat to a pole held parallel to the river by piled stones, moved back into the stern to fill the tea pail.

"Mostly, Doc, the boats along the Peace are tied up to this north shore," I heard him remark to the anthropologist who was shouldering a duffle bag. "The starboard side catches most of the sun, and that's why you'll find seams opening there first. By jove, this is the longest I've gone without tea since I freighted airport supplies to Fort Nelson along the Sikanni. That river is so muddy we finally had to carry drinking water."

We slept that night beneath conifers through whose rustling needles stars blinked. When I awoke the next morning, King was approaching the rejuvenated fire with a wide-bottomed shovel which he proceeded to clean by thrusting it into sand. His back was politely toward me as I wriggled into brown woolen slacks while still beneath the eiderdown, and I watched absently as he shoved the tool into the blaze. He removed it finally and performed some sort of a hidden operation. I soon smelt bacon and heard eggs sputtering.

"That's a new one on me," Doc chuckled, appearing with towel and toothbrush. "Custom around here?"

"Forgot the frying pan," King grinned, making motions

with a stick. "I don't know if this shovel isn't an improve-
ment at that. The long handle is sure handy."

Haze lifted, as the day warmed. We thundered more
deeply among towering bluish peaks. Little white streams
danced down. High meadows were bright green patches.
Glaciers sparkled. Then, directly ahead, waves thundered
and heaved.

"Parlez Pos Rapids," King identified colloquially. "The
real name, I guess, is the rapids Qui Ne Parle Pas—the rapids
that do not speak. They don't give any warning when you hit
them from the other direction. A stranger coming downstream is right on top of them before he knows it. We'll be up
through them in a minute."

The boat yawed, creaked, plunged, and once a wave
curled lustily aboard when the propeller raced terrifyingly
in space. I saw the wet blackness of tumbled boulders appearing in a sudden vortex. Then power straightened us as
King swung the rudder, and we surged into quiet water.

We stopped to refuel where a sulphur stream was a milky
flow. Rocks were laminated with layer after layer of fossil-
ized sea shells. Cliff swallows had built their homes along
the banks, some in eroded yellow peaks like penthouses. Cut
banks showed deep beds of water-rounded gravel, covered
by one to several feet of loam. Once a bear lifted its dripping
snout from the water, rared up, and then fell over backwards
in its anxiety to scramble away.

"There's a cave for you, Doc," King gestured late that
morning.

"I don't think it'll do," the other smiled. "No one could get
to it without ropes, could they?"

"Not as a regular thing, anyway," King admitted, glancing
again at the high dark opening north of the river. "That's the
Cave of the Winds. It's certainly changed history of this
Peace River country."

"How come?" the other asked.

"Indians have always been afraid of it as far back as we know," King explained. "Even today, they'll hide in the bottom of your boat when you pass here. That's so the evil spirit they think lives up there, and howls when there's a wind, won't notice them. They never would travel through here by themselves. Why, there isn't even a trail through this Peace Pass. There's trails through the Laurier and Pine Passes on both sides of here, though, and they're both a lot higher and rougher than this. I've driven horses through here, and so has Skookum Davidson. There's nothing to it."

We camped for the night beside the lacy torrent of Wicked River. Arctic grayling and rainbow trout, at the line where the crystal stream and the turbid Peace mingled, bit so avidly that they often didn't even wait for our Black Gnats to dimple the surface before striking.

"That's Mount Selwyn opposite," King motioned. "That cave we were talking about in Hudson Hope is up there. It's the only one I know of that might fit your description, Doc, except for some gravity caves near Brad's and a couple of shallow limestone openings two miles further up the Canyon from there. We can go along to Finlay Forks tomorrow if you want, climb Selwyn the next day, and return to the Hope the third."

He looked at Doc, and Doc glanced inquiringly at Brad, and Brad turned to me.

"I'm just along for the ride," I said weakly.

"Well, it's not likely I'll be this far again," Doc decided to my delight. "I'd like a look at Finlay Forks."

We ran the Finlay Rapids, too, keeping close to the left shore whereas we'd held nearer the right of the first chutes. The greyish green Parsnip River ebbing prettily from the south and the muddy Finlay River roiling down from the north met ahead in the great continental trough that lies west of the Rockies and east of the Wolverines. Thus, we saw, was the Peace River born. Henry Stege's old trading post and a few other deserted log buildings were about, marking the remains of a former settlement. We curved toward the present trading and outfitting outpost of Finlay Forks which now lies a few miles up the Finlay River.

"When a railroad is eventually built through to Alaska," King Gething noted, as we surveyed the flat valley arrowing northwards between tremendous ranges, "it'll probably run along here to Whitehorse. There was a lot of agitation to build the Alaska Highway along this route, you know."

"How come they didn't?" Doc asked.

"The snow averages four or five feet deep along the Finlay here, for one thing," King replied, wrinkles curving about shrewd dark eyes. "When I used to siwash up here winters with the mail, I had to break out a new snowshoe trail practically every trip. Where the Highway is now, you know, it's comparatively semiarid. Well, Brad, you can see from which direction the Peace gets its color."

"A lot of it comes from these Finlay mud banks, doesn't it?" Brad noted. "But where does it pick up this whiteness?"

"That's from White Water Creek, or Milk Creek as we used to call it, about a hundred miles north," King said, swinging the bow to avoid one of the many stranded dead trees known as sweepers. "It originates where the Lloyd George Glacier is grinding up white limestone. The surface of the particles is so great compared to their weight that they remain in suspension."

"I suppose you could identify most of these streams, couldn't you," Doc asked, "just by the color?"

"Well, of course, it varies some in different stages of water," King allowed. "The Omineca is sea green, you might say. The Nation is light brown. The Pack is dark brown. The Ingenica is glass clear. Sometimes, you know, the two colors don't mix for maybe three or four miles after a junction. The Crooked is like weak tea, which reminds me, by jove."

A full moon was yellow among the mountains when we returned to our camp at Wicked River. The aurora polaris shimmered in a sky still stained, along the serrated horizon to the west, with red traces of the departed day. A breeze, softly warm against us, was accentuated by our almost gentle progress. I moved up forward beside Brad who was sitting intently in the bow.

"Isn't it exquisite?" he murmured, making a place for me. "And tremendous! It's just the sort of rugged hunting and fishing trip Vaughn and Roy Heffner would thrive on."

"Yes," I said, "and it could be kept easy enough for our mothers, too. I wish they were with us now, don't you?"

Brad nodded.

The four of us started early up Selwyn, the highest mountain along the Peace River. Once a mother duck and five small ones diverted us, bobbing down a silvery cascade at one side of a brook and then paddling up the main current to shoot the chutes again and again. The trail became steeper. Quartz and schist rattled underfoot. We reached a point at noon where what seemed to be a limitless cloud-bound sea of peaks and glaciers extended in every direction.

"The way to the cave is down a bit and then up again," King said.

It lay, a shallow and gaping forty feet square, at the top of a great rock slide. Marmots whistled as we climbed to it, and there were the deer-like tracks of mountain sheep.

"You're right, it's another gravity cave," the anthropologist agreed. "You can see how the roof fell out and just slid down the hill. Not much use to dig here. But, say! Even if that had been the toughest trip in the world instead of the easiest wilderness trek I've ever been lucky enough to take, this sight would be worth every minute of it."

Water trickled from two perpetual snowbanks into a glacial lake, beside which we'd already kindled a cooking fire where the blackened tea pail was even now steaming. The mountain pool, sublimely transparent even when the high free wind chortled low enough to facet it, was such an extraordinary sapphire that all at once I had the impression that it, too, was an untouched and nearly forgotten relic of prehistoric ages.

The wind seemed like time itself, flowing past us in a great unbroken stream, and it was almost as if Thoreau was noting for the first time that a lake is the landscape's most beautiful and expressive feature. "It is earth's eye," Thoreau seemed to be remarking, "looking into which the beholder measures the depth of his own nature." As long as Brad and I live in the wilderness, I felt myself vow, we'll never dwell away from water.

CHAPTER TWENTY-FIVE

MEAT FOR THE HUNTING

Poplars became bursts of flame against incredibly blue skies. It felt good to be back in our wilderness home. The first frost came in September, the night we returned from the river cruise. Although warm sunny weeks steamed after it, the snow cones of the higher Rockies steadily became whiter and more imposing.

Gene Boring loaned us Cloud and Chinook in return for the use of Brad's carbine. It would be possible for us to own these two horses, we found, for $80. Large as that sum seemed at the moment, it was less than what we had paid for weekly canters along the Fenway the previous summer. The grey gelding and the sorrel mare were fast and rugged, sure footed and well broken. We wished we had that much cash now.

Two old saddles, plus bridles and other gear, Brad got from Gene by swapping him ammunition and other belongings. The trading occupied most of a day, and Gene drove Phyllis and their children up for the occasion. Duffle bags that hadn't been disturbed for months were dragged out. Boxes were taken down from storage shelves.

A certain amount of tension seemed to exist between the men at noon, giving Phyllis and me opportunity to explore

King Gething and four bear that had been destroying his
buildings and food cache.

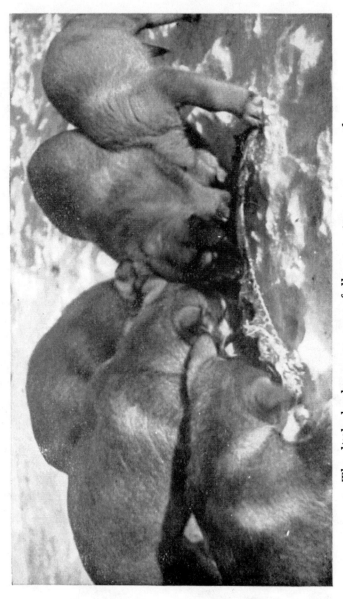

The little husky pups peacefully gnawing on moose-rib.

across the dinner table such subjects as how moosehide gloves are cut and how some women actually use sphagnum moss instead of diapers. By supper, however, both Brad and Gene were conversing so elatedly that we women could only listen.

As a result of the formula of barter the two of them glowed with the pride of achievement. What one doesn't want, trading principles seemed to decree as nearly as I could figure, one should praise ingratiatingly. This, incidentally, makes the owner glad he still owns that particular item. What one really desires, however, he accepts only reluctantly. This, of course, leaves the original possessor correspondingly glad to be rid of it.

"Hasn't this been a nice day?" my husband beamed when we came back indoors after waving good-by. "Well, let's examine the loot. Say, I'm glad we're rid of that tent. We'd never have used the thing."

"Phyllis said Gene was sure relieved to get shed of that big old saddle he got from Ted Boynton a year ago," I remarked innocently.

"What's the matter with this saddle?" Brad demanded. "It'll ride just like a rocking chair. Oh, it's maybe a little heavy, but I've always wanted a saddle like this one. Say, isn't that little job I got for you cute?"

The saddle he had obtained for me was neat and pretty, I had to admit, stroking its smooth brown surface. Although it and the other articles bore the well oiled aura of long and respected use, there seemed no question even to my inexperienced eye that they all were substantial, too.

Our first sustained attempts at western style riding were so rough that I was soon glad we could at least escape the added conspicuousness that new leather would have evoked. On city bridle paths, we'd learned to sit the English saddle with its short stirrups that are particularly well adapted for jumping. We adjusted ourselves to a trot those days by posting, as everyone called it, which meant rising from the saddle at every other bump.

"Humph," Dennis Michitee once said, watching with less than the usual amount of Beaver Indian calmness a guest of Joe Barkley riding a somewhat bewildered cow pony Eastern style. "Big daylight all the time under pants."

Westerners, we soon learned, took advantage of their large comfortable saddles which are built for long hours of work and sat out a trot. It proved difficult to accomplish this without, as Dudley expressed it, riding off in all directions. Finally, by sticking to it until we were too sore to repeat the same mistakes, we got the feel of leaning relaxedly back and absorbing the jar by using our loosely flexed knees and thighs as springs.

These cayuses could pick their ways at gallops through bush where we'd have hesitated to walk their metropolitan cousins. Food bills were nonexistent. They kept fat at the ends of regularly moved picket ropes.

Hardwoods along brook and river exchanged their greens for warmer colors, and by contrast the several little Christmas trees near our windows seemed more like emerald cones than ever. Gradually from week to week, the character of each poplar and birch came out, and it admired itself in the shrinking mirror of the water.

Mists that lifted from the river, now near its low water mark, became grey and heavy. They swirled downstream in the morning like the gay hurrying ghost of ancient voyageurs, anxious to get Outside before freeze up. Brad brought in the bear rug, and it felt softly warm underfoot. The atmosphere seemed to take on an alertness. The green blanket before our windows became worn and tattered, and Mother Nature's patches grew increasingly gay.

I could see why Thoreau spoke of cranberries as "small waxen gems, pendants of the meadow grass." Ours became plump and red, although they seemed tiny when compared to those we'd seen growing near Concord's Walden Pond. The bear didn't seem to mind, however. We saw repeated evidences of how they were gouging themselves with every sort of fruit, reenforcing their already rotund bodies with additional fat for the long winter's sleep.

High bush cranberries we picked, too, although I could never arouse any prolonged enthusiasm in Brad for gathering berries except for his immediate consumption. We liked their refreshing sourness. When I plopped one in my mouth, I thought ahead to how good they'd soon taste, scarlet and frozen. Thimbleberries were prolific, too. So were blueberries. It was exciting these days to roam the woods with bags ready for whatever we could find.

"What kind of a winter is it going to be?" we asked King Gething when we rode through the bush to his coal mine on Bullhead Mountain.

"Well, I don't rightly know," King admitted, dark eyes twinkling as he hooked a pipe from his mouth. "I asked an Indian that question the other day. He said, 'Oh, plenty bad winter.'"

"How could he tell?" Brad asked.

"What he told me," King responded, "was, 'White man got big wood pile.'"

Brad worked at odd hours in tightening the cabin we'd reserved for a cache, our north woods storehouse. We stored our crop of potatoes, cabbages, turnips, and other vegetables in the bins there beneath the floor. The wood pile, too, required an increasing amount of attention. Brad made a game of felling the pines needed for quickly firing kindling and the poplars that promised quiet, sustained blazes. He set stakes in the ground and attempted to drive them out of sight with the trunks of the giants he toppled.

It looked like so much fun that I tried it with some smaller trees; standing far enough back to estimate the center of weight, making a shallow cut low on the side of the trunk where I wanted the timber to fall, and then plying the thin-bladed Swede saw on the opposite side a few inches higher than the first cut until creaking and snapping fibers warned it was time to yell, "Timber!" My trees were small enough so that I could guide their descent to some extent by pushing, which only evened up, I argued, for the fact they had such a comparatively narrow striking area.

"How much more interesting an event is that man's supper who has just been forth to hunt the fuel to cook it with!" Thoreau enthused.

I came to agree with him. These days I did not want to decrease our mounting wood stacks by even one stick, and I was continually scouring the nearby forest for fallen limbs. "A few pieces of fat pine were a great treasure," he had determined a century before. I could understand how he'd felt, particularly when I wanted to prepare a quick meal with a short lived blaze that would not make the cabin too hot.

"Every man looks at his wood pile with a kind of affection." Any such sentiment had seemed remote when I had considered it in our Back Bay apartment. Now I sensed there is a fierce instinctive satisfaction in proving one's self truly self-sufficient that most city folk never have an opportunity to savor. As surely as food and shelter meant life to us, so did that wood pile in this northland.

"I loved to have mine before my window, and the more chips the better to remind me of my pleasing work. They warmed me twice, once while I was splitting them and again when they were on the fire. No fuel could give out more heat."

Swans clamored southward, peopling the woods with the sound of a larger life than they could longer sustain. Their clamor filled me with a strange exultance not matched by that aroused by the thin, throaty excitement of migrating geese, ducks, and of hundreds of sandhill cranes that moved through blue skies in great chalky streaks.

Day by day, the river became lower. We could finally pick out one deep narrow channel that wended among gigantic rocks, past gravel and sand bars, and through ledges. Evenings we liked to walk upstream, going down the nearest cut bank immediately to the now wide shore and leaving this only to cross overland around Box Canyon.

Here, interestingly enough, we could follow for several hundred yards an ancient canyon eroded from rock centuries before when the Peace or some other river had followed another route. We sometimes contemplated sinking a shaft for gold that perhaps lingered there in old gravel, but we knew we'd never do it. Similar nearby operations had only resulted in loss of time and often astonishing amounts of promoted capital.

What panning I had done so far had netted only a few flecks of gold. Even the gravel bar nearest to where we'd seen the bear and her two cubs had not produced more than several yellow specks a pan. There were no nuggets here, only a trace of dust. Hard long work might have paid me a dollar or two a day, which was what the few remaining gravel punchers managed to gross on some of the better bars upriver. Secretly, I was just as glad. There was enough gold in the world, I decided. The unspoiled wilderness bred far less trouble. Besides, I'd accumulated grain by grain enough raw gold with which, sometime when we were Outside, Brad had promised he'd have a ring made for me.

One morning we started early and reached the Gething mine in the middle of original Rocky Mountain Canyon. Transportation difficulties had closed this Aylard operation years before. A tall log cabin, built by Jack Adams for Les Aylard, was long used by Larry Gething as a trapping cabin before he sold his line to Charlie Ohland who continued to utilize the handy shelter with its bed and stoves.

The coal seams at this spot had first been discovered by Sir Alexander Mackenzie. We stared at tremendous dinosaur tracks in the rippling sandstone near where that explorer had camped. When we tried to proceed further up the canyon, sheer cliffs soon barred our way. We could see why the savage water had always forced boats to portage or to turn back.

"If we ever make it all the way through the canyon," Brad admitted, "it'll have to be on the ice."

"Everyone says we never could make it."

"Everyone except the Gethings," Brad qualified. "They claim we might be able to do it if we get the right kind of winter."

The Peace River rose sharply the middle of October because of storms at the headwaters. The current that had cleared to a sparkling green jadeite translucency became murky once more. Freezing nights followed in rapid succession now. Rain and wind tore at the trees. The opposite slope became almost bare except for conifers. Only a few yellow leaves fluttered from the hardwoods.

Grazing became more and more limited. Cloud and Chinook stayed fat because we used them only sparingly and because we changed their picketing areas as often as every hour. Unless we were going to feed them, however, we realized they should be let loose to shift for themselves. We were unusually quiet, I guess, when we put bridles on them that last morning and rode them bareback down to Gene Boring's.

"Must be good feed up there," he noted, running a hand over their sleek sides. "They'll winter in fine shape. I saw the herd down at the spring just this morning."

Chinook's ears were alert when Brad slipped off her bridle, and then I heard a whinny in the distance. The sorrel mare answered. Finding herself free, she angled away in a trot that flowed into a gallop. Cloud hesitated until Gene slapped him on the hip. Then he followed Chinook after one long backward glance.

"The little beggar," Brad breathed, gripping my hand tightly. "I'm going to miss that redhead, too. What she hasn't got in brains, she makes up in spunk. It'll seem empty around the cabin awhile without them."

"Meat will keep now," Brad noted on the way home. "It's time we start hunting in earnest."

He got a mule deer up above Box Canyon and a young, bull moose in a swamp a half mile behind the cabin, so close he was able to skid it to the cache in four trips. He shot a big bear, and I rendered more than twelve quarts of pure white grease which lived up to its local reputation by proving at once to be a far better shortening than any commercial product I'd ever tried. When I wasn't busy, I went out with the .22 after grouse. They were fat and delicious this time of year.

We awakened one morning to find the ground white with snow.

"Here's our chance," Brad said, hurrying through his chores. "We're going to need one more moose if we hope to have enough meat to last the winter. You'd better grab that carbine I got back from Gene and come along."

The day was softly beautiful. The snow made everything look different, as if our world had been enchanted. We eventually cut fresh tracks on the plateau a mile inland from the cabin. Even I could see they had been just made.

"Probably a bull," Brad decided. "See how it dragged its feet? Cows generally make a neater imprint. And look here. Instead of going through those spruce, it went around. That could mean it has antlers to watch out for."

"What'll we do?" I whispered.

"It's feeding into the wind. Notice how the tops are nipped off those young poplars? It's probably been sleeping. Sure, look there." The sight of the depression made by a great reclining body sent a thrill through me. In the hollow several coarse, dark brown hairs were frozen. "It may be lying down again by now."

"Well, what'll we do?" I demanded more urgently.

"That will pretty much depend on what this trail tells us," he responded, studying the terrain with his binoculars. I waited breathlessly, suddenly conscious of the dark cold gleam of the .250-3000 under my arm. "Let's follow these as quietly as we can for awhile. If we scare this fellow and start him running, we may never get him. Keep watching all the time."

The fresh uncrusted snow allowed us to proceed almost without noise, and I found I could feel the hardness of sticks under my feet in time to set my weight where there'd be no warning snap. Once the trail veered directly west toward where we knew a creek canyon lay. Assuming the animal would not descend from the height of land at this time of day, Brad gambled by heading again into the north wind.

When we cut the moose tracks once more, two wolves were following them out of a coulee. They looked like gigantic sled dogs until I saw their yellow elongated eyes. By the time either of us thought to shoot, they were zigzagging away through the bush. Brad tried to get a sight on them, and then, remembering the moose, he lowered his gun without firing.

"Doggone," he said, so tense that his low-pitched voice was unsteady. "They must have weighed about 180 pounds apiece. What a pair of broken-field runners those fellows would make! A bullet would be a lot easier on this moose than those hamstringing savages would have been."

The spoor indicated that the moose had still been ambling along and feeding when it had passed here. It had paused and turned occasionally to survey its tracks, but it had still not noticed anything dangerous. I thought of the moose skeletons we'd seen at the mountain lake. The wind was cold on our faces. Snow swished gently as it fell from trees and bushes, often to melt down our necks. The tracks began to zigzag.

"Easy," Brad whispered, hauling me close beside him in a squatting position. "He's figuring on lying down. Before he does, he'll probably swing back in a half circle. That's so he can watch his back trail. He can depend on his nose and ears to protect him to windward."

"What'll we do?" I asked for the third time that morning.

"Their eyes aren't so much except on moving objects," Brad considered. "Their ears are extremely keen, though. So are their noses. This fellow has probably swung back into the wind far enough so that he'll smell anything close on his trail, even if he doesn't hear it or see it first. Well, he isn't apt to hear us in this sort of going."

I shifted my weight from one heel to the other, as Brad studied with his glasses the park-like flat. Widely spaced poplars were enlivened by occasional clusters of willow and patches of spruce, tamarack, and juniper. Brad looked back at me.

"The best thing," he said, "is for you to keep going into the wind. Don't get very far ahead of me, honey. I'll stay on the trail, and you'll be able to spot me most of the time. You'd better jack a cartridge into your barrel, and be ready to shove that safety off in a hurry."

The big animal must have got Brad's scent, for it couldn't have been ten minutes later that it burst with an unnerving clatter from a thick clump of spruce. It stood broadside not a hundred feet away, never seeing me. Great nostrils worked as it drove air explosively from its lungs again and again and inhaled searchingly. A tremendous pair of antlers glistened in the sun. I remember trembling for Brad to shoot. The moose started to trot away, and then I guess I realized desperately that the spruce must be in Brad's line of vision. I discovered, too, that I'd been holding the carbine to my shoulder all this time and that the safety was off.

My single shot through the heart gave us over five hundred pounds of rich red meat. Only afterwards did I start tc shake. By then Brad was hugging me and slapping me on the back.

"Your first moose!" he was shouting. "We eat! Boy, oh boy, oh boy!"

I made myself think of steaks, roasts, chops, barbeques, mulligans, mincemeat, soups, and juicy charred kabobs.

CHAPTER TWENTY-SIX

ARE MEN THE BEST COOKS?

The Hudson's Bay Company says so. In its cookbook prepared for post managers, the Governor and Company of Adventurers of England trading into Hudson's Bay state unequivocally, "The best cooks in the world are men."

I suspect this statement may be inserted largely as a morale builder, because a few sentences further along the potential world's finest chef is cautioned not to use his dishcloth to wipe off the stove.

Yet the majority of good cooks in the North, certainly, are men. Some visiting sportsmen never completely recover from the spectacle of hairy-armed sourdoughs lounging about a trading post and swapping recipes.

These old timers go in mostly for plain cooking, although occasionally you'll meet a bannock puncher with a flair for the exceptional. One of these, of course, is Ted Boynton. Rotund Ted, who's cooked for the Harrimans and other millionaire dudes on sheep and grizzly hunts, has long been famous as one of the best trail cooks in the continental northwest.

That's why I was particularly happy when, for five dollars, Ted came up with his horses and little yellow dog and skidded to our cache the moose I'd shot. I decided I was going to get some pointers on cooking. I did, too. What Ted Boynton accomplishes with rice, Vesta Gething who's a wonderful cook herself had told me, is enough to assure his popularity with any pack horse outfit. Hewn down to indoor proportions for my benefit, Ted's favorite recipe goes:

"Hack up two onions and a fist-sized chunk of sow belly. That's salt pork, Vena. Brown 'em a mite in a kettle. Add a quarter cup of water and two cups of rice. Boil rice until soft. Don't do no stirring, for cripe's sake.

"Excuse me. . . . Well, er, be heating a half can tomatoes, a teaspoon of salt, and maybe a tablespoon of celery salt if you got any handy. Add these to the cooked rice. Sprinkle on cheese like . . . like aitch. Then you sure don't want no lost dudes wandering into camp for awhile."

The most sybaretic outfit Ted Boynton ever hoisted a frying pan for was the Charles F. Bedaux expedition. Bedaux, at whose French chateau Wallis Simpson and the Duke of Windsor were married, had crossed the African desert with five passenger cars. He estimated that it would be a comparatively easy matter to ride tractors through the Canadian Rockies above Hudson Hope.

Bedaux set out with five tractors, 130 horses loaded largely with gasoline, and enough kitchen paraphernalia to outfit a Jasper Park hostelry.

"Why now, if I'd ever tied into all them fancy kettles and such, I never would have got anything done," Ted admitted to Brad and me. "Bedaux didn't give an aitch, though. So in my spare time, I showed him how small an outfit a bush cook can get along with."

The internationally renowned efficiency expert was most interested in the way Ted split Arctic grayling up the back and then pegged them flesh-side-out on heated birch slabs. These Ted leaned close to a small fire, occasionally turning them end for end. When the fish became flaky, there were individual hot plates all attached.

"Bedaux never did get through these mountains with his tractors, did he?" Brad asked curiously.

"Nope," said Ted, "he lost just about his whole outfit. But he sure learned how to plank a fish."

There are a number of ways to cook without dishes, I've found. Some of them save one the trouble of carrying utensils on short trips. Indians, for instance, sometimes heat water in containers made of birch bark. These can't be placed over the fire, as Beth and Charlie Brent and Brad say they tried once in New Brunswick. The trick is to drop hot stones into the liquid.

Dough, I'd learned shortly after my arrival, can be wound around a heated peeled stick and baked over hot coals. Steak, besides capable of being suspended over coals in numerous ingenious ways, can be grilled between two hot stones. A whole meal can be steamed in an earth-sealed hole with wet grass between the layers of food and the hot stones at the bottom.

A surprisingly effective way to cook small game is started by encasing it in about two inches of clay that has been worked with water until it's like stiff dough. This is covered with embers. If the bird or fish is a small one, it may be removed in a half hour. When the shell-like covering is broken, any feathers or scales will peel off with it, leaving all the sealed-in juices and flavor. A two or three pound trout, we've found, takes three-quarters of an hour. A large salmon, for example, requires correspondingly longer.

Jolly Ted Boynton had one of his hardest workouts when he went into unexplored Mackenzie River regions with Harry Snyder, sportsman prominent in helping develop Canadian uranium deposits. Accompanying scientists, who took pictures of musk ox and gathered hundreds of museum specimens, had Ted cooking all the wild edibles he could find.

"I guess they reckoned they had me stopped proper.

though, the day they lugged in a brace of mud hens," Ted chuckled. "I remember how Mr. Snyder allowed he'd tried mud hen before. He said that if the part he got went over the fence last, somebody must have given it a boost."

Maybe it was the odors sifting into the atmosphere from the direction of Ted Boynton's fire. Maybe it was just curiosity, for a mud hen—although kind to its family and all— is generally about as tender and tasty as a discarded moccasin. Anyway, there was no second call that evening to the pan-banging accompanied: "Come and get it."

There those fowl were, browned and bulging, looking as handsome as canvasbacks and smelling certainly no less tempting than fat ptarmigans. At least, that's how a bushman who accompanied the party describes them. George C. Goodwin, American Museum of Natural History mammal collector, stuck his fork gingerly into a drumstick. Moist steaming meat fell away from the bone. Everyone dug in hungrily.

"Even a loon don't cook up too bad," grinned Ted, "if a yahoo don't try to gentle it aitch-for-leather. So don't throw any of such critters away, particularly in times like these. Cram them with onions. Boil real easy for three hours. Then start brand new with a crumb stuffing, tuck a mess of sow belly where it'll do the most good, and roast nice and quiet like. Well, I reckon Bingo and me have got to be heading along. Where's that dog? Bingo, you get to hell away from that moose!"

Pinned down the next mail day to name the one thing we missed most in the wilderness, Brad and I decided that it must be ice cream. That was when Bill Carter told me how to make our own in a few moments with snow.

Light dry snow is best for the purpose, Brad and I verified that very evening, but almost any clean snow will do. The manufacture is as simple as it is speedy. You merely empty a can of evaporated milk into a pan, then add sugar and flavoring. Vanilla extract will do for the latter. So will cocoa. Something like wild strawberry preserves will satisfy both purposes. Then you step outside and stir in snow to taste, sampling periodically. The result is delicious.

"The white man's frying pan," Mr. Gething asserted that same day, "has ruined a lot more Indians than firewater."

Bob Yeomans, Stanley Wallace, Billy Kruger, Vic Peck, and other sourdoughs have told us the same thing, and I guess it's doubtlessly true. This cooking weapon should be used sparingly, particularly when loaded with grease. It is probably the most abused of all cooking utensils.

"A lot of city sportsmen," Brad put in from the vantage of having recently been one himself, "feel that when they go hunting and fishing they've got to rough it and cook everything in a fat-ladened skillet. I don't know if that's roughing it or not. It's really making it rough for themselves, though, isn't it?"

"That's right," Mr. Gething agreed, and Vesta nodded sympathetically.

A good way to cook steak, my husband impressed upon me a few days after our marriage, is in a hot frying pan without grease at all. Fat meat will provide its own lubrication, anyway. Good cooks already know this, of course, and I'm certainly not going to pose as a member of that sorority. Too many who'll read this have stopped at our cabin for tea which, in the North, means anything from a banquet to just beverage.

You always invite any passerby in for tea. This is a logical custom in a country where distances are great and where society, therefore, is all the more treasured. The fact that Brad and I naturally are in Hudson Hope a lot more than anyone there is up our way keeps us embarrassingly, although pleasantly, ahead on the exchange, a shortcoming we try to make up for in other ways.

To come back to Indians, religious taboos often restrict these aborigines' already inadequate diets even further.

"No eat 'em whitefish," Dokie, one of the Moberly Lake Indians traveling with Harry Garbitt, shuddered recently when he saw the trader cooking up some of the fish Dokie regards as his blood brothers. "Whitefish me."

"Okay," Garbitt, who was journeying light, acquiesced dryly. "Supper's over."

There is on the other hand a ridiculous side to the white man's dining habits, particularly in the eyes of the native who makes it a habit to eat whenever hunger prompts him.

"White man crazy," King Gething says an Indian remarked to him one day up river. "White man look at watch to see if hungry."

Dudley Shaw, what with all the culinary talk, set out to prove during the following week his long-avowed contention that the backwoods wife needs no maple tree to provide her with maple syrup. A credible substitute is started, Dudley insisted, by boiling six medium-sized, unpeeled potatoes with two cups of water until but one cup of fluid remains. The potatoes are then removed from the pan, he noted conservatively, ready for the table.

While I stirred the liquid until the boiling peak was once more reached, Dudley carefully added one cup of white sugar and another of brown. Once both had entirely dissolved, we set the saucepan on the back of the stove.

"Aw," Brad, who'd been busy writing some sort of a letter, grunted disappointedly after stealing a spoonful, "you're going to have my wife doubting that men really are the best cooks. That doesn't taste like anything, Dudley."

"Ghastly stuff," Dudley nodded agreeably. "Like home brew, it has to be aged in a dark place. After a couple of days in a bottle, it'll be noble."

"Well, I don't know," Brad allowed doubtfully, sealing the letter without offering to let me see what it was about.

"It sounds farfetched. Why should potato water and sugar taste anything like maple syrup?"

"I never could figure it out," Dudley agreed. "Do you want me to mail that letter for you in case you don't prowl to town this week?"

"Thanks," Brad said, and I didn't even get a glimpse of the address before Dudley stowed the envelope in a pocket. Now that I thought back, this sort of thing had been going on for several weeks. "Potato water and sugar! It sounds like one of Charlie Brent's tall stories about when he was a red-nosed boy in Oklahoma."

Doubtful myself by now, I nevertheless followed Dudley's instructions. Brad and I forgot about the bottle until the end of the week. Then Brad happened upon it when searching under my bunk for paper with which to wrap some negatives we were mailing out that day to be processed. When he sampled the elixir this time, his face took on an amazed expression. Spoon refilled, he turned to me.

"I never would have believed it," he marveled. "Here, Vena, try this."

"No!" I said, so we both tried one more spoonful. "No, it can't be true."

"Doggone," he admitted, "I guess I owe Dudley an apology. The concoction does taste almost exactly like fine maple syrup. Who says the best cooks in the world aren't men?"

"Not me," I replied weakly.

Dave Cuthill didn't exactly superintend what went on in the HB.C. kitchen that afternoon. By this time, however, I wouldn't have been surprised if he'd appeared any moment in chef's cap and apron and taken over. David Moody Cuthill it had been who'd first pointed out to me that sentence in the Hudson's Bay Company manual which, even if somewhat ambiguous when you considered it, did aver that the best cooks in the world are masculine.

Even if Dave didn't superintend the actual work that particular afternoon, it seemed only natural that he should appear from time to time to make sure that everything was progressing favorably. The rest of the time he spent in the living room where Brad, except for an occasional rumble of conversation, was engaged in answering another letter I wasn't allowed to see.

"If they won't give us some action down there," I heard Dave assert once, although it didn't make any sense to me, "we'll get in touch with Victoria. I'd better close this door."

I didn't have time to venture into the living room, anyway. I was too busy helping Marion prepare one of the aromatic Hudson's Bay Company Christmas Puddings that—traditionally varying according to what ingredients may be on hand—have crowned many a holiday feast in the farther places since the world's oldest trading corporation was founded nearly three centuries ago.

My assignment wasn't as difficult as it was confining. Now I finished sifting four cups of flour, then painstakingly checked off items as Marion dropped them into the great yellow bowl she was using.

"Four teaspoons of baking powder," I repeated. "Half a teaspoon of nutmeg. Half a teaspoon of, what's that— uummm, cinnamon. A quarter teaspoon of cloves. One cup of brown sugar, and a half cup of white sugar. Any potato water?"

"What?" Marion asked.

"Dudley showed us this week how to make an imitation maple sugar," I explained. "It's good, too. Do you want me to stir?"

Marion added two cups of minced moose suet from a quarter we had sent down with Ted Boynton, a half cut of diced mixed peel, two cups of raisins, and a cup of finely chopped dates. My arm began to ache, so I broke in the two eggs the recipe called for and splashed on a teaspoon of lemon extract. Then Marion reverently stirred.

Dave appeared, glanced over the situation until Marion stopped to rest her arm, then disappeared rapidly back into the other room. Marion, with an expressive twist of her mouth, continued the ritualism by tipping in a libation composed of one cup of browned white granulated sugar melted in a little water. She then poured in what she described as enough milk and worked the mixture deferentially into a cake batter.

Heavy cotton was at hand for the pudding cloth. Marion wrung out the fabric in water. I sprinkled it with flour.

"Hold it tight," Marion bade. "Don't let it get away from you. I'm going to pour in the batter."

Only a little bit spilled. We shifted hands as cautiously as possible. Marion held the bulging pudding cloth. I bound its gathered top with half hitches according to instructions from Dave who with Brad stalked in purposefully on the way to the post office, otter hat angled over one brow.

"Leave enough room," Dave urged, "leave enough room. That sweet scion of the haggis is going to swell, by God."

Brad, because of an argument advanced by Dave that as potentially one of the world's best cooks by authority of the Hudson's Bay Company cookbook he should be accorded a role in the ceremony, was allowed to lift the cover off an already steaming kettle.

The pudding was immersed in the bubbling water where it started to boil for what Marion, cautioning Dave at least to remind her of the time, trusted would be no longer than three hours. The process resulted almost at once in a tantalizing odor whose provocative aroma increased the longer Brad and I remained. But that was the last either of us saw of the pudding until Christmas.

CHAPTER TWENTY-SEVEN

THE RIVER STILLS

Our newly completed cache was pleasant with bunches of wild onions, spicy white yarrow, dark amaranth seeds and dried wild peas, and such potherbs as Indian lettuce and sunny mustard blossoms. Greenish brown leaves of Labrador Tea promised many a steaming cup.

Dandelion roots, to be roasted and ground for coffee, had withered until they humorously resembled toy dragons. Reddish flowering-dogwood inner bark, for stretching any dwindling tobacco supplies, was becoming more aromatic by the week.

There were such essentials as sugar, too, and baking powder, and plump bags of flour bulging cozily between suspended wires. Great haunches of meat, delicately marbled with fat, promised many a sizzling chop and succulent roast. Everything we needed, I thought again to myself, including one another!

The terrestrial music of the wind began to throb around the cabin in deeper earnest. Cold howled down on the last day of October, ending our swimming and our outdoor bathing. Like Thoreau, I poked the fire with more satisfaction than usual.

City existence, with its grimly assertive amusements for

an unamused multitude, had habitually become deadly with the boredom of nothing to do. Here I discovered my fall days interestingly occupied by small tasks, such as making arnica by soaking the golden blossoms of that native flower in mail order alcohol.

There was a feeling of accomplishment, too, in compounding mustard by mixing the crushed seeds of wild black mustard with flour and vinegar. Although I'd never liked sewing before, my very needle seemed to flash a smile as it made the smoke-tanned pliableness of moosehide spell mitts for Christmas presents.

The fact that we were barely earning our keep did not worry me as much as it had once. What if the income from our writing should be even as tardy as Thoreau's had been? The longer we lived in the wilderness, the better I could understand and appreciate the soundness of his philosophy on that subject.

"By working about six weeks a year, I could meet all the expenses of living," he had found. "For myself I found that the occupation of a day laborer was the most independent of any. The laborer's day ends with the going down of the sun, and he is then free to devote himself to his chosen pursuit."

I turned over in my mind, as Thoreau had before, other money-making possibilities in the wilderness. They included guiding, outfitting big-game hunting parties, arranging fishing and river trips, hunting for bounty, prospecting, making rustic novelties and perhaps building up a mail order business for marketing them, trading, lumbering, freighting, buying a trap line or making arrangements to trap on shares, and berrying. "I also dreamed that I might gather the wild herbs."

The voice of the river began to soften. One morning the first week of November a skim of dark transparent ice extended from shore to shore across the quieter stretches of the Peace. The sun never reached many portions now, and ice here held its own throughout the day and thickened further during the lengthening cold hours. Coyotes began to follow the smooth rim.

The brook froze several days earlier. A sharp blow with the heel was all that was needed at first to break an opening through which we could dip our pails. But on November Four, Brad had to come back for the ax.

"If you want to see something pretty," he invited, "let that berry pie go for now and come with me."

Cutting through black translucent ice, he opened a window at our feet. Kneeling impulsively, I looked down into what Thoreau had called, "The quiet parlor of the fishes." It was pervaded by a softened light as through ground glass. There a perennial, gently moving serenity reigned as in the twilight sky.

"'Heaven is under our feet,'" I said, "'as well as over our heads.'"

"Thoreau was right about a whole lot of things, wasn't he?" Brad mused, tilting the pail so that it would sink and then lifting it, dripping with pure crystal water. "It's easy to understand why he answered as he did on his deathbed, isn't it, when someone asked him if he'd made his peace with God?"

"'We have never quarreled,'" I quoted softly. "That really describes his way of living, doesn't it? I'd like to read more about his life sometime. Outside of an occasional passage here and there, we never have read anything except *Walden*, have we?"

The deep and almost snowless cold that descended suddenly remained. The river froze over at what natives said was an unusually low stage of water. It did not break up again as commonly occurs. Instead, seeping and solidifying overflow made the icy pavement all the smoother.

"Maybe this is the year Brad and I will be able to walk

through Rocky Mountain Canyon," I casually suggested one afternoon to Dudley, occupied once more with problems of baits, traps, and cunningly improvised snares.

"Don't try it, Vena." His eyes blinked with sudden earnestness behind their thick spectacles. "Tons of water pile down there so fast the blinking ice is never good, not even where there is ice. Besides, you'd freeze your lugs."

"Didn't a survey party get through?" Brad asked, looking up from a bottle of scent with new interest.

"With vast quantities of ropes, help, and luck," Dudley nodded. "If either of you fell in that current, you'd be bogged down for good. There'd be no chance of getting out of those whirlpools and that torrent, even if you didn't get swept under the ice. No one else ever made it through that frightful maelstrom. Indians from away back have always shunned the notorious place."

"I thought it was the Cave of the Winds up near the head of the Peace that kept Indians off the river," I said. "The Gethings say that when Indians were in their boats, they'd lie down when passing the Cave of the Winds so evil spirits wouldn't see them."

"The Canyon, too," Dudley declared emphatically. "The Indians warned Mackenzie about it. They were right, too. Mackenzie was the first man who ever prowled overland all the way to the noble Pacific. But he had to leave the Canyon a little way above the old mine and hack a portage trail over Bullhead. Even Mackenzie couldn't make it through that ghastly congestion."

We were soberer than usual that dusk when we returned Dudley's "Cheerio," and watched him move out of sight down the trail.

"Maybe we would be foolish to try it," I thought aloud.

"Maybe," Brad nodded soberly, "but the Indians are afraid of a mere hole in the mountains, too. Now what could be dangerous about that Cave of the Winds? Maybe we ought to take their characters into account before deciding anything. We don't have to make up our minds now. What do we know about them, anyway?"

A lot of the trappers who trade with humorous and casual Harry Garbitt at Moberly Lake to the south, with keen affable Teddy Green in the Graham River country to the north, and with the Hudson's Bay Company in Hudson Hope are Indians. These red hunters of the white snows aren't the alert and stalwart aborigines of story books, I knew. Too often, I realized, they're thin chested, frail, and indolent in the white man's ways they've patiently adopted—the remnants of a race that is following the last long trail which mastodons and saber-tooth tigers traveled centuries ago.

"They don't get the right grub," Fred Monteith, an old settler, smouldered one day when the Beavers were at Hudson Hope to collect their five dollars apiece in annual treaty money from the Dominion. "Plenty of rare fat meat, all parts of the animal, would give them every mineral and vitamin. But it's easier to eat the white man's free pork and flour."

"It's the same everywhere up here, isn't it?" I had asked.

"Yes, it's this way with Indians and Eskimos all over the North," Monteith had nodded. "They spurn their old foods and their old ways. That only makes them more susceptible to the white man's diseases against which they haven't any racial immunity, at best. Why, it only took measles to wipe out a large part of the Moberly Lake population a few years back."

Free cod liver oil, vital in these regions where the sun supplies adequate Vitamin D only three months per year, is too often wasted by Indian recipients we know who use it to feed dogs and to oil harness. Cough syrup, when quantities were dispensed without charge by the Indian Department, was found by one agent being lavished indiscriminately on pancakes. Such liquids as liniments are apt to be drunk unless personally administered by the doner.

"The easiest way to beat competition in trading furs with an Indian? It is to give him whiskey," Henry Stegie, who used to trade up river at Finley Forks before opening a store at Hudson Hope, told Brad once. "It's also the worse way if you want to keep doing business under the same tree."

The several dozen traders we've met very, very seldom resort to liquor except at the most to invite an Indian friend to join in a courtesy toast during some holiday. Indians, all of them contend, just cannot handle liquor whether in the usual commercial forms or in the substitutes occasionally accepted by white sourdoughs. These latter include lemon or preferably vanilla extract, some of the most unbelievably caustic liniments which after locker room experiences with them Brad can't even abide on his body, and a red ink shipped north because of an alcohol base which afforded it resistance against the cold. When many an aborigine touches liquor, he'll trade almost anything for more. One eventual outcome is that he won't have enough possessions left to enable him to keep his family even in necessities.

There have been a lot of explanations about why an Indian cannot hold liquor. Part of the answer, I think, must lie in their imaginations. One Treaty Day when Lloyd Gething who later organized the Peace River Coal Mine was just a youngster, he set up a refreshment stand at Hudson Hope and sold root beer. The earthen jar very definitely contained nothing but freshly made root beer, manufactured repeatedly on the spot by the simple expediency of adding powdered flavoring to well water. The business Lloyd did, however, was amazing. Indians who clustered nearby and drank nothing but the root beer were soon staggering happily all over the road.

The unventuresome northern Indian, like all uneducated peoples, is also held back by his superstitions. The Crees here fear such a simple act, for example, as the burning of green spruce boughs. Such a deed, they believe, will bring deep snow. Cree children are cautioned against tossing pebbles into Moberly Lake, lest they annoy the water spirits and cause dangerous waves. Northern Lights are believed to be the ghosts of the dead. If one whistles outdoors when the aurora polaris is wavering above, Pat Garbitt told me, it is whispered that the specters will try to snatch you into the heavens.

It's actually harder to keep from making *bad medicine* than to pick up a working knowledge of the euphonious Cree language. The vocabulary contains only about 600 basic words. The some 30,000 others are combinations. We began to pick up some of the simpler words and phrases as soon as we arrived.

Dudley Shaw, for example, talked of the wapoose. It wasn't long before we realized that this is the name for rabbit, which here isn't actually a rabbit but a varying hare. Ted Boynton spoke of mooswa which, of course, is moose. Muskwa, Charlie Ohland translated in the middle of a conversation, is bear. Jennie Ohland, his energetic and friendly little wife, wondered at the same time if the Cree word for cat doesn't have a European origin. It's poos. Amisk, which Dave Cuthill asserted is the backbone of many a local trapline, is beaver.

The verb in the Cree tongue often forms a complete sentence. Tense, mood, subject, and predicate may all be included in one word by means of prefixes and affixes. There are other simplifying factors. In English, for example, we speak of young sheep as lambs, young deer as fawns, and so on, often with several synonyms for each. Crees can merely add the diminutive "little" to the regular noun. A baby hare, leveret, or tiny bunny is in Cree merely wapoosoos or little rabbit.

Liquids are dealt with in as casual a manner by adding "a-poo" to the name of the object from which the fluid is derived. So-min is grape. Wine, therefore is so-min-a-poo. It is a pleasant, gracious language, becoming a graceful and intrinsically dignified people.

The Indians much publicized sense of direction actually exists, we found, only in his own neighborhood and of course in fiction. The white man who works at it is a far better woodsman than the Indian, the sourdoughs we know agree. This general difference exists everywhere between educated and uneducated races. All one has to look at for proof is the records of explorers. Peoples fear what they do not understand, and the uneducated races understand less. It's probably as simple as that.

Racial education has nothing to do of course with intelligence, poise, and native wit. Lillie, the octogenarian son of a chief who is regarded by Teddy Green as the finest gentleman this certainly discerning trader has ever known, more than held his own a few summers ago with some field men from one of the world's greatest museums.

The scientists' conversation was good humored enough and maybe, as such things often unconsciously are, a little envious. Did Lillie have a separate teepee for each squaw? Were his fingers and toes sufficient for the task of counting his papooses? All Teddy Green could courteously do, except for an occasional vitriolic innuendo, was bite down on a chunk of bannock as eloquently as possible. The museum men, singularly unsuccessful at baiting the old Indian, finally began to unpack rods and fly cases. Were there any fish in the Graham River, one of them asked?

"No fish," Lillie regretted, dark face as sober as ever. "Big water last spring. Fish all drown."

Lillie, although much too polite to show it, has more of the traditional contempt for the egotistical tenderfoot one occasionally meets than does any other Indian we know.

"Can I reach Hudson Hope by this trail," Teddy Green once heard a self-important dude inquire of Lillie, although a survey party had been thoughtful enough to mark Hudson

Hope on a tree and to add an arrow pointing in the correct direction.

"Maybe," Lillie allowed with studied care. "You try!"

The cold intensified even more, as winter neared. Unlike Thoreau, we were not troubled by deep snow. Like him, we seldom allowed any weather to interfere with our roaming abroad. His experiences therefore seemed the closer to us, although a century away, when we read appreciatively: "I frequently tramped eight or ten miles through the snow to keep an appointment with a beech tree, a yellow birch, or an old acquaintance among the pines."

Our tiny brook was bewitched early this December to a broad icy lane which we followed into its own deep canyon two miles inland from the cabin where the waters ebbed from what seemed like our own private springs. Owls were resting there in afternoon shadows, awaiting the dawn of their day.

The temperature was 16° below zero when we arose on the first day of winter. It had lifted only three degrees by the time sun came into sight at half-past eleven. There was no wind. Every bush, sapling, and conifer within sight of the windows sparkled with frost.

"Today's the day we select our Christmas tree, remember?" I said when Brad eyed me inquiringly from the typewriter, as I pulled on outdoor clothing.

"Is it the Equinox already? Time certainly races by up here." He laced on his outer pair of moosehide moccasins, then scuffed into rubbers while buttoning a kersey stag shirt. "I've got one picked out for you to pass on."

"Is it symmetrical?" I asked, that being the characteristic most difficult to discover in this country where young evergreens grow by the thousands.

"Oh, sure," he nodded. "It's standing pretty well by itself on the river bank."

"Aren't you going to take the ax?" I suggested.

"Oh, I don't know as we'll need to take it," he replied.

"Why," I asked doubtfully, "is this tree pretty far away?"

"Well, it's not too far," he allowed. "As a matter of fact, there it is right in front of you."

"But that . . . that's right in our front yard." I looked to see if he was joking, but his eyes were serious and even, I thought, apprehensive. "We don't want to chop that down, do we?"

"Do we have to chop down our Christmas tree?" he asked, eyes intent on mine. "I've sort of been wondering. . . . Well, there won't be anyone in our cabin on Christmas to get presents from our tree."

"Isn't that all the more reason to keep up the tradition?" I asked, throat tightening despite my answering resolution to be sensible.

"Sure," he went on, less confidently now. "I was just figuring. . . . Well, I wondered if we wouldn't get more of a kick out of it if we shared it with the folk who are already here? Instead of a lot of gaudy stuff that doesn't mean anything," he plunged on, "well, why don't we use food for decorations? Oh, I guess it isn't much of an idea."

"But it's a wonderful idea!" It took a few moments for me to exchange the visions I'd had of a tiny spruce standing trim and nostalgic inside our log home for the suddenly blurring picture of a living Christmas tree. Why, of course! Why hadn't I thought of it? I wiped my eyes, as plans seemed to mist in front of them. "Let's see, I could string chains of cranberries. The birds would like those."

"How about some suet pendants for the red squirrels?" Brad asked deferentially.

"Yes, yes. And I can make some little tinfoil cones and fill them with crumbs. Oh, it's wonderful." I lifted my face enthusiastically, and he soberly kissed me. "I'd like to start right away. I won't have to bother you at all."

"Say," he said with mock protest, "I'm in on this, too, remember?"

Decorating our living Christmas tree proved so much fun that I forgot to start dinner in time. Brad was topping the little spruce with a crowning star he'd cut with sudden inspiration from bacon rind when, an hour late, I lifted the boiled potatoes off the stove and gave our sizzling moose sirloins their final turn. As we ate, we laughed at the greediness of two grey Canada Jays who discovered the offerings almost immediately.

The sun, beaming through the four windows touched the sixth log of our north wall. The eaves kept its direct heat out of the cabin entirely in summer, but now it so lifted the temperature that I cheerfully let the fire die to a mass of embers.

As the sun disappeared at 4:04 P.M., the final rays touched with holiday red a little flock of feasting snowbirds. Other birds, squirrels, and even a sharp-eyed ermine so enjoyed sharing our yuletide that with a lump in my throat I resolved to keep waste scraps of food there the year round.

Twilight deepened with a great serenity into a night brightened with stars, moon, and the Northern Lights. We'd been dreading the short dark days of winter, but they were proving incredibly restful. We made birch bark cards to send to city friends. As Christmas neared, both Brad and I became increasingly occupied with strange tasks that seemed to cease abruptly when the other approached.

CHAPTER TWENTY-EIGHT

SUBARCTIC CHRISTMAS

A wolf was howling somewhere down river in the frosty blueness of pre-dawn when we arose early the day before Christmas. Its voice lifted and lowered, rose and fell and soared another time in three crescendos. The last of these wavered away before reaching the pitch of the first two. There was echoing silence, and then the wolf repeated its wild aria.

Brad, taking a birch bark horn left from efforts of the past moose season, went outside and impulsively answered the lonely call. Stillness closed down again. It seemed the more intense because of the muted thunder of cold-jollied land, ice, and trees. Then the wolf once more lifted its predaceous muzzle to the azure heavens. Brad answered anew, and one more time the wolf howled its twelve-arpeggio plaint.

"What kind of a day is it going to be?" I asked when Brad came in rosy-cheeked and smiling.

"The wind's the wrong way," he said, "but the sky seems crisp and clear enough. We ought to have a fine walk down to the Hope. When do you want to leave, Vena?"

"Oh, any time," I said looking out to where feasting snowbirds already embellished our living Christmas tree, "so long as we get there in time to help decorate the Cuthill's tree tonight. You know, I almost wish we weren't going, Brad. It would be so perfect to spend Christmas here by ourselves."

"Do you feel that way, too?" he asked with growing pleasure. "I thought you'd want to be among people for the holiday."

"I thought you'd want to be."

We laughed, and I smelled the wind-sweet freshness of his flannel shirt suddenly cool against me.

"Well, it'll be fun," he said. "It'll certainly be something to remember, too, spending Christmas at a HB.C. trading post. When I was young enough to write letters to Santa Claus, I remember addressing them in care of the Hudson's Bay Company, North Pole."

The Peace River was so solid that we walked all the way to Hudson Hope on the ice; an unusual occurrence for that time of the year, Ted Boynton told us when we met him skidding a barrel of water from the big spring halfway up from the landing. A sub-zero wind whistled through our woolen clothing as if it were burlap. We walked backwards occasionally, holding momentarily unmittened hands against our faces, but we felt glowing and exhilarated.

At Dudley Shaw's when we stopped at Sunnybank to enjoy his heater and where we munched raisin bannock and sipped tea to better the occasion, our nearest neighbor said he'd see us in the Hope on Christmas morning.

"All the old sourdoughs who can stagger that far will be prowling to town," he chuckled. "Everyone enjoys vast conviviality that day and downs copious amounts of lap."

"Tea?" I asked.

"Not on Christmas," Dudley replied.

King Gething, helped by several excited youngsters, was stringing wire from the HB.C. electrical system to the school when we emerged over the brow of the trail from the river.

"Got to have lights for the tree," he explained. "By jove, it's nippy, isn't it? We'd better go over to the house for a spot of tea with Vesta and Dad."

The Peace River directly above Pcx Canyon.

Cabin on Alaska Highway at Kluane Lake.

After the celebration at the school that evening, where Fred Monteith was a jolly Santa Claus and everyone received presents, we went back to the Bay. Marion, Dave, Brad, and I put presents under the little green spruce that glistened from our efforts with tinsel, baubles, and a great silvery star.

"A lot of people nowadays," Dave remarked, settling back in his chair, "listen to Dickens' *Christmas Carol* when the tree lights are on. I've always liked the less known accounts of Robert M. Ballantyne. He was apprenticed to the Hudson's Bay Company at the age of sixteen. The stories he wrote led many another lad to join the 'Adventurers.' "

"Dave, included," put in Marion.

"That's right," Dave Cuthill smiled, and he picked up a small old volume. "Here's an account Ballantyne wrote about Christmas in 1843 at York Factory, one of our trading posts. See if you could have resisted him either."

When David Cuthill commenced reading, his words took me back beyond that holiday which had taken place only fiften months before Thoreau borrowed Alcott's ax and started building his home in the woods. My mind teemed with visions of beaver skins, inaccurate maps, stockaded towns, fur-heaped Indian canoes, waving fleur-de-lis banners, buckskinned white adventurers, and great flaming campfires that silhouetted the animated figures of bartering traders and redskins.

I thought back to the occasion in a Boston inn when Pierre Radisson and Medard Groseilliers, whose fortunes in furs had been twice confiscated in Montreal by the sly governor of what was then New France, met Sir George Carteret who took them to London to meet his king. Boston, somehow, always managed to weave an integral thread throughout the warp and woof of northern destinies.

A trial voyage to Hudson Bay by the English ketch Nonsuch under master Captain Zachariah Gillam, of where else

but the same Massachusetts capital, must have lived up even
to some of the pair's more extravagant promises. Nearly one
hundred thousand dollars worth of furs was brought back to
London.

"When it shall Please God to bring you thither," the old
orders to the Boston master had read, "you are to saile to
such place as Mr. Gooseberry and Mr. Radisson shall direct
you within the Bay and there endeavour to bring yor. said
vessells into some safe Harbour in ordr. to trade with the
Indyans there and you are to deliver unto them the goods
you carry. . . ."

The ketch returned with its wild cargo in October 1669.
The Hudson's Bay Company—on May 2, 1670—was given
the exclusive right by King Charles II to trade in an incredibly rich wilderness that later proved to be larger than all
Europe. The parchment charter caused many to spend their
holidays in these farther places during the intervening centuries, I thought, and I recalled Winston Churchill's recent
Christmas greetings to those of the HB.C.

"The Hudson's Bay Company is the oldest chartered company in the world, and its life has been filled with achievements of which you may be justly proud," Mr. Churchill had
said. "Yours is a fine record of enterprise in opening the ter-
ritories of North America and in serving their peoples. In
sending you my good wishes, I am glad to recall the fact that
John Churchill was its third Governor."

David Cuthill's voice was droning on, and my mind returned with an effort to Ballantyne's version of an HB.C.
yuletide in 1843. Brad was sitting rapt, I saw, and Marion
with a leg curled absorbedly beneath her was gently rocking
and sewing. My eyes strayed to the presents beneath the tree
then back to our host's clear ruddy face and his light eyes
now intent on the volume in his hand.

"The table was covered with a snow-white cloth whereon
reposed a platter containing a beautiful fat, plump wild

goose," David Cuthill read, "which had a sort of come-eat-me-up-quick-else-I'll-melt expression about it that was painfully delicious. Opposite to this smoked a huge roast of beef, to procure which one of our most useless draught oxen had been sacrificed. This, with a dozen of white partridges and a large piece of salt pork, composed our dinner. . . .

"At the top of the table sat Mr. Grave, indistinctly visible through the steam that rose from the wild goose before him. On his right and left sat the doctor and the accountant, and down from them sat the skipper, four clerks, and Mr. Wilson, whose honest face beamed with philanthropic smiles at the foot of the table. . . ."

"After the feast everyone adjourned to the hall where a scene of the oddest description presented itself. The room was lit up by a number of tallow candles stuck in tin sconces round the walls. On benches and chairs sat the Orkneymen and Canadian halfbreeds of the establishment, in their Sunday jackets and capotes.

"Here and there the dark visage of an Indian peered out from among their white ones. But around the stove the strangest group was collected. Squatting on the floor sat about a dozen Indian women, dressed in printed calico gowns. Colored handkerchiefs covered their heads, and ornamented moccasins decorated their feet; besides which, each wore a blanket in the form of a shawl.

"They were chatting and talking to each other with great volubility, occasionally casting a glance behind them where at least half-a-dozen infants sat bolt upright in their tight-laced cradles.

"All this flashed upon our eyes, but we had not much time for contemplating it. The moment we entered the women simultaneously rose, and coming modestly forward to Mr. Wilson, who was the senior of the party, saluted him, one after another, a custom of the ladies on Christmas." Concluded Dave, chuckling, "And a bonny custom it was, too."

"Is that so?" his wife said with uplifted eyebrows.

Some sound alien to the wind-heaving insistence of the night awoke us early, and Brad to whom holidays were usually just another day seemed as eager to tiptoe downstairs as I. Marion and Dave, looking guilty, were already surrounded by ribbon, boxes, and wrappings.

A beautifully crude little heart, carved by Innuits from prehistoric mastodon ivory that had probably been preserved for centuries in some Arctic ice bed, was the Cuthill's gift to me. For Brad there was a letter opener made of the dewclaw of a moose, encased in an intricately beaded moose-hide sheath.

When I came to our personal presents, I had to laugh, only the laughter changed to tears. Brad had traded his carbine for Cloud. There was a bill of sale in my name, mounted in a birchbark frame with my favorite snapshot of the grey gelding.

"Aren't you going to say something?" he demanded.

"Open y-yours," I managed to stammer.

When he tried on with proper enthusiasm the gauntleted moosehide riding mitts I'd sewn for him, he discovered a wad in one thumb hole. It was a bill of sale made out to him for Chinook. I'd bought his favorite sorrel mare with $40 of my article money.

"Gosh," Brad said, almost as inarticulate as I. Then he blurted softly, "Gosh, no wonder I love you."

"No wonder I love you, too!" I heard myself whisper above the sudden noisy concern Marion and Dave seemed to be evincing in gathering up paper. "Merry Christmas, dear. Merry Christmas, everyone!"

Guests began arriving for the customary Christmas imbibitions, and soon we all left to make the rounds of the Pecks, Gethings, McFarlands, Ellises, Kyllos, Pollons, Rutledges, Boyntons, Borings, MacDougalls, Ohlands, and the other local inhabitants. Harry Garbitt was in town, and so were Dudley

Shaw, Bill Carter, Bill Keily, Gunnar Johnson, and some more so-called old timers; none of whom seemed at all old. Everyone was in the utmost of good spirits, whether toasting the occasion or not. Nothing had happened to the registered mail sacks this year.

Pillars of smoke from log cabin chimneys of the northern settlement seemed to be supporting the nacreous roof of mist that shimmered above the pulsating land on cold days such as this.

After a dinner topped off gloriously by the steaming aromatic HB.C. Pudding, we heard the silvery bells of the horse herd. "A patch of snow inhabited by barbarians, bear, and beaver," was how Voltaire acidly described the North two centuries ago. He should see a Hudson's Bay Company trading post today, I thought, as Marion searched out carrots and apples for me from among her bulging supplies. Brad appeared in the kitchen, and we went out together to greet our new possessions.

"What a wonderful present!" I enthused again, arms around the gentle neck of my very own horse. "To think of all the times I've wished I owned a horse! And to have Cloud!"

"I kind of like Chinook, too, you know," he grinned at me. Then he said, "I thought sure you'd guess weeks ago you were going to get cloud."

"How could I possibly guess? Besides I was trying too hard to keep from letting you know about Chinook."

"I suppose that is what kept you stymied. But did you think I'd get those saddles and other gear just for borrowed horses? Say, no wonder Gene wouldn't even talk deals for an option on Chinook." He chuckled. "As a matter of fact, I'd planned another present for your real surprise. Nothing's come from my letters yet, though."

"Oh, what is the other present going to be?" I begged, but he just rubbed Chinook's ear and smiled. "All right, don't tell me. I'm sure I won't like it one umpteenth as much as I do my horse?"

"Oh, no?" he asked with a strange definiteness, and his smile deepened.

There was the customary community dance that evening, and then we gathered in the Cuthill's snug living room for one final ritual—the toast to those far away. There were many "absent ones." Some eyes misted, but not for long. Here were friends. Here was the nugget moon under which the friendly frost-rimmed roofs of Hudson Hope glowed like opals. Here was the wild, free wind.

CHAPTER TWENTY-NINE

ROCKY MOUNTAIN CANYON

Brad and I weathered some merry gales and spent cheerful days close to the fire, while occasionally sparse flakes of snow whirled wildly without and even the hooting of the owl was hushed. The larger blaze became a friendly watchdog in its barrel-like kennel, snapping and growling at wintry temperatures.

The remainder of December and all January continued cold and nearly snowless. Wolves howled nearby, although they habitually left the river to avoid passing in front of the cabin a hundred feet above them. Moose herded near our log buildings as if for safety. Enjoying their presence, we never disturbed them. Sometimes when we saw the great humped forms silhouetted against the low winter sun, their glossy dark coats seemed golden.

When frost lay heaviest, not even Dudley visited our wilderness home for weeks at a time, trusting us to advance in his behalf from understudies to stars in the never ending drama at this end of his trapline. Like Thoreau, we lived in the whitened forest "as snug as a meadow mouse." The almost bare ground made for easy walking. We welcomed the lack of snow. As for the cold, it was spectacular and exciting.

River and brook overflowed nearly every February night.

Where the ever moving current dropped over the center of our dam, however, Bull Creek remained open. It was an odd sight to see Brad sidling into a narrow rift in ice taller than his head. As he dipped each bucket in the gurgling stream, he'd hand it out to me. Once our rubber pail was torn out of his mittened hands by the force of water and was swept under the ice between dam and waterfall. It took him all one afternoon to trace the channel and chop it out.

The brook's overflow froze almost as fast as it appeared. It moved like a glacier nearer and nearer the cabin in a solid, rounded wall. Our pole bridge had been hidden several weeks before, and we had to wear rubber on our feet whenever we crossed the always wet stream.

"You know, I've never seen the ice so smooth," Mr. Gething told us one mail day when the two of us sent out no less than five new articles, the weather being so ideal for concentration. "I was born in 1866, and I came into this country back in 1900. I've never seen ice like this before."

"Do you think we could make it through the canyon?" Brad asked.

"If you ever can," Mr. Gething allowed, "you should be able to do it this year."

After two false starts, one in late February which was halted by deepening cold and another in early March when what looked like an approaching storm made us reconsider, the weather turned warm. Chinook followed chinook. Open gashes appeared in the river, and more water than ever sparkled atop the ice.

"Let's head out now," Brad said abruptly one afternoon. "We'll stay at the old mine tonight and push on through tomorrow if we can."

"I've only a half loaf of bread," I hesitated. "I was going to bake more tomorrow."

"That'll make a couple of sandwiches apiece. Why don't I mix together a waterproof bag of flour, baking powder, sugar, salt, and raisins. Then we can add water and make bannock as we need it." He considered. "Some moose kabobs, tea, and enough oatmeal and butter for tomorrow morning should see us through. There'll be a pot and spoons at the mine cabin for breakfast. All we'll have to take is a boiling kettle—this tomato can will do—and a couple of our stainless steel cups. All right?"

"All right." I started to slice the bread. "How about raspberry jam and peanut butter for sandwiches? I've maybe a dozen oatmeal cookies, too."

"Good," he nodded. "We'd better wear those high rubber-bottomed boots. It's pretty wet underfoot, and we may hit snow where the canyon narrows and deepens. We can keep a fire going in the mine cabin tonight, so we won't need bedding. You'd better hang this sheath knife on your belt just in case, and we'll take along a coil of rope."

"And the Leica," I added.

"The camera, definitely," he agreed, "and sun glasses. We may as well shove a few of these little adhesive bandages in our pockets in case any blisters start."

"It sounds like a real expedition," I bubbled.

"It stopped Mackenzie," Brad said with some grimness, "and Mackenzie was quite a lad."

The river ice, bright and glaring, was so slippery that we shuffled rather than walked. Sometimes a rough portion would afford purchase, and we'd make a short dash and then slide laughing for breathtaking yards. The sun was insistent now, but probably no more so when men with ropes and paddles had sweated beneath its glare those other days when Sir Alexander Mackenzie had rested scarcely long enough to note that the huge pearl-green poplars where our cabin now stood were the largest he'd ever seen.

Iron-stained cliffs confined the reflected warmth, and we did not rebutton our shirts even in the shadows of Box Canyon. When we passed close to the mouth of Deep Creek a half mile farther upstream, there was a shallow trickle of muddy water and a noise that puzzled us until we discovered its source. Jagged stones were thawing from the acute V of cut banks above. The smaller of these spun menacingly through the air, growling and snarling, to bury themselves in a house-high drift that slides had amassed below.

"Right here is where Mackenzie camped one night," Brad was saying. "Over across, atop that high bluff, is where he saw elk. Up there is where his men argued again that they should turn back."

"That the discouragements, difficulties, and dangers, which had hitherto attended the progress of our enterprise, should have excited a wish in several to discontinue the pursuit, might be naturally expected," Mackenzie had written in his diary. "Indeed, it began to be muttered on all sides that there was no alternative but to return. Instead of paying attention to these murmurs, I desired those who uttered them to exert themselves."

Explorers had been trying for centuries to find a way across North America. It went back to Columbus's encountering America when he was really looking for India. Adventurers, dismayed to find the New World barring their way to Asia's riches, sought a practical trade route to the Pacific.

Balboa crossed the narrow fever-plagued Isthmus of Panama in 1513. The Spaniard was the first known European to see that the blue Pacific lay beyond. Sir Francis Drake, English pirate, repeated the exploit. He studied the Pacific from the crotch of a tree.

"Almighty God," prayed Drake, "of Thy goodness give me life and leave to sail once in an English ship upon that sea."

But all this had happened far, far to the southward. For three centuries all attempts to cross the main North American continent were unsuccessful!

The search for a road to the Pacific began in earnest when the French fur trader, Verendyre, and three sons set forth with a canoe brigade from Montreal in June 1731 in an effort to pierce the wide green wilderness. Misfortunes multiplied. Thirteen years later, the two remaining brothers stood with a war party within sight of towering mountains which they wanted to climb in an effort to glimpse at least the western sea.

The painted Bow Indians with them, fearing an attack, would not linger. François and Pierre Verendyre had become the first white men to see the northern Rockies. But a thousand miles still lay between them and their quest which that day ended.

Alexander Mackenzie, personable 27-year-old Scots fur trader, had early wrested a fortune from the Canadian wilderness. At his Fort Chipewyan trading post on Lake Athabaska, in what is now Alberta, he debated whether going up the Peace River to the west or down the same current would lead him to the Pacific. He canoed downstream and sensed only failure when he reached the Arctic Ocean on July 15, 1789, after mapping the continent's longest waterway, thereafter called the Mackenzie River.

He headed westward four years later up the Peace. It was when he reached Rocky Mountain Canyon, where Brad and I were now, that progress became almost impossible. Despite Indian warnings that no one had ever been able to traverse the 22-mile chasm, Mackenzie continued on up river instead of carrying his supplies across the portage that approximates the present one from Hudson Hope.

When paddling no longer availed, men lined the canoe up through thunderous waters, walking precariously along the edge of precipices and pulling a long rope which was attached to the 34-foot craft in the whitened river below.

"Even Mackenzie couldn't get beyond this point," Brad said the next morning.

I should have been sleepy, for it was scarcely dawn even atop the cliffs one thousand feet almost straight up. A rising wind had hissed all night through the squared logs that had twisted with the years, and whichever of us happened to be awake had to arise about every hour to drop fresh fuel in the upended gasoline drum that served as a heater. It had seemed as if I'd lain sleepless, although occasionally I'd been aroused by Brad's crawling back beside me when I couldn't remember his leaving. I felt keenly awake now, however, and almost ominously tense.

Snow was in the wind this morning, heavy as damp feathers, but we were continuing anyway. We'd passed the dinosaur tracks now hidden by ice and dark collapsing tunnels which had followed coal seams back under the mountain. We were beyond the mine flat that bristled like a giant prehistoric porcupine with fire-stripped trunks. Cliffs heightened and narrowed, and there was the thunder now of open rapids that churned nearly from bank to bank.

The river as far as they could see, Mackenzie had recorded, was one white sheet of foaming water. When the canyon could be followed no longer, he and his men hauled the canoe over Bullhead Mountain. They had struggled up the extreme slope we were regarding now. A trail had been chopped so that the trees formed a sort of railing.

"There may be one of them," Brad indicated. "It's a pretty dry climate, and the Gethings say you can still find evidences of the old trail. There's another, maybe. Well, we'd better start moving."

The deepness of the snow that pulled at my leg muscles showed that sun and chinook seldom invaded this narrow twisted fastness. Occasional pits revealed where rocks had torn down from overhead. There was no way here that we could walk out beyond the danger line, and we kept an eye on the often overhanging crags from which dust occasionally fluttered into the cold depths below. Once we sprang back from a slide that left a drift at our feet ugly with half-buried shale. Swinging as closely to the edge of ice as we dared, we hurried past.

"Are we going to be able to make it?" I wondered aloud.

"I'd hate to turn back now," Brad said.

We rested at a bend where the torrent had worn a wider passage through its rocky prison. Vein after vein of black coal, some yards wide and others only thin dark streaks, lay exposed on both sides of the river. There must have been at least fifty of them at various levels.

"There's a fortune in this wilderness," I thought aloud, "if they ever get a railroad."

"Maybe there's enough fortunes in the world," Brad commented, "and not enough wilderness. How's about a drink of water before we move on?"

He lay on his stomach and dipped his mouth into the current. After a moment, I followed suit. Water pressed into my eyes and nose before I could suck up a mouthful. Then I gasped and laughed. It was full of invisible ice particles that tickled my throat.

We cut ourselves poles from driftwood. We had to leave them when a projection of water-tormented sandstone required the full use of our hands if we were to edge along the precarious crevices its very instability afforded. We tied the rope between us then. But although Brad might have been able to anchor me in case of trouble, I imagined he secretly realized the doubtfulness of my ability to hold him.

"Use your knife in a hurry if you have to," he called back at one point when shale dislodged beneath his feet, and I had no more doubt of it.

We reached ice again. No more wood was in sight. Snow became thicker, blurring even our ribbon-like glimpse of the outside world between the precipices overhead. At one time we saw the almost perfectly chisled head of a dog jutting from the rock above. Despite the din of boiling water and the whistle of gale-driven snow, the scene with its absence of ordinary noises seemed heavy with a sort of silence.

"The Silent Places," I thought to myself, and remembered again our first night in the woods.

At one place we had to crawl on our stomachs along a narrow strip of ice with rushing black water below and a clay-ironstone buttress undercut by erosion only inches above. We looked back from where the river swung southwards for a few yards. I could see that the same eddy, lowered by winter, had been eating at the ice. Only a shell had supported us.

"Phew," Brad said, "I don't want to have to go back over that."

I looked upward.

"Yes," he said, following my glance, "no one can climb out of here, either."

Progress became slippier and more difficult. The sting of hardening snow pellets caused me to resort to sun glasses which I soon had to remove, however, because of the darkness of the canyon bottom. I wanted to hurry, and yet there was a fascinating magnificence here that made me feel impelled to linger. Along one stretch there was nothing to do but wade across submerged boulders. The water, fortunately, did not reach the tops of our heavily greased boots.

Far more appalling, though, was where Brad who was leading had to scale an abrupt and nearly smooth spur of rock. A film of frozen spray on the farther side halted him, clutching for purchase. Knife in hand, he leaped to slanting ice beyond. Because of the angle, I had no way to anchor him without surely pulling him into the cataclysm that seethed inches away. I shouted. He stopped his terrifying slide toward open water by driving the point of the hunting knife into the ice. Then he actually waved nonchalantly. I was trembling, as I followed.

"You're okay," he called. "I've got the other end of this rope twisted around a rock."

I couldn't stop shivering, and holds seemed to dwindle away.

"What's the matter?" he asked when he flung his arms around me to stop my skidding descent a moment after I'd jumped. "The rope would have held you all right from this end."

"You shouldn't have taken such a chance."

"What else could I do?" he asked. "Besides, I knew I could stop sliding by using that knife. I had all the time in the world, too. You didn't see me hurrying and losing my balance, did you?"

"No," I admitted weakly, "but I wasn't worried just about your sliding. That piece of ice is about to break away from shore, that's all."

When we had worked our way around that next bend, he looked back to where the flow was washing the eroded and half-toppled sheet. His mouth tightened wryly.

"I never thought of that," he said.

Wind drove more furiously into our faces. We passed a series of low ice caves, made by springs dripping from ledges. Then the acute walls on both sides started to flatten. Ahead was an iceblink, the white glare near the horizon of ice-reflected light. I saw mountains in the distance. In a few moments I recognized the tangle of boulders and potholes at the canyon's narrow mouth. There was an old Gething cabin near where an ancient trading post had once stood. There was the gash of the portage trail.

Here, I realized was where Mackenzie had once more launched his canoe. Here his weary and often mutinous crew had started paddling again through the very backbone of the Rockies, from where they'd pushed on across the Great Divide. For the first time since Columbus had happened upon the New World 301 years before, North America had been crossed north of Mexico. The first of all explorers had reached the Pacific Ocean by the overland route.

Mixing red pigment with grease, Mackenzie had written in large characters on the southeast face of a rock this terse memorial: "Alexander Mackenzie, from Canada, by land, the 22nd of July, 1793."

So had we succeeded on our minor journey, I thought, tired but immensely exhilarated. I remember boiling the kettle, and I recall the sweet oily blackness of birch smoke. But it was in a sort of anesthetized langour that we trudged back along the fourteen-mile portage trail to Hudson Hope. We stopped there only long enough to pick up the mail, for we felt like being alone. I didn't want anything to shatter the almost too real unreality of this mood. Five of my children's stories had sold, I learned, but today it was just another circumstance to be vaguely accepted. There was a check for me for one hundred dollars.

The night air seemed to have a dreamy gentleness matched by the tranquillity of the now clear blue sky. A warm chinook breeze once more wafted snow, like dew-laden petals, from the always fragrant garden of trees about the trail.

A goose honked in nearby velvet darkness when we were halfway home. Several arrived early each year, Dudley had said, to nest on the islands in front of his cabin. It was close to March, I realized languidly. We had been making our home in the woods for a year.

CHAPTER THIRTY

ALASKA HIGHWAY

Thus was our first year's life in the woods completed, to paraphrase Thoreau, and the next three years were similar to it.

Why did we even consider leaving such happiness? Perhaps it was the persistence of relatives. Perhaps it was the urging of friends who told of the great opportunities, mostly financial, that we seemed to be missing. Perhaps it was the clangor of swans heading out of the north that fourth autumn. Perhaps it was because of what Thoreau had written, for Thoreau had been so right in everything else.

"I left the woods for as good a reason as I went there," he said. "It seemed to me that I had several more lives to lead, and could not spare any more time for that one."

Our writing had been going encouragingly well—well enough certainly to buy us, in exchange for a few hours' work most mornings, everything we reasonably wanted. We'd also helped a few sportsmen, who'd written us after reading our articles, to arrange fishing trips up river and big game hunts in the mountains. One party of three had just returned in fact with a full bag of sheep, goat, moose, and even a grizzly apiece. That sideline had occasionally given us a little extra pocket money, although unless a lot of preparations were entailed we generally were glad to share in planning such vacations just for the very real pleasure of it.

Brad had even found time to complete two hundred typewritten pages of *Home in the Woods*, the log cabin book he had spoken of writing when first arriving in the bush. We'd had lots of fun with it so far, trying to get down on paper many of the kinks we'd observed or tried firsthand and which, as far as we know, have never appeared in any other book. He had expanded its scope, mostly because of my urging, and had subtitled it: "The Art of Living in the Woods."

We'd sold among other things more than a dozen pieces about the nearby Alaska Highway, most of them on order. We seldom wrote on speculation any more, preferring to save waste motion by querying first. We hadn't even traveled the engineering epic except for the sixty some miles between the railhead at Dawson Creek and the turn up the north bank of the Peace River. So we decided to go out that way.

Vesta Gething suggested we'd get a more realistic perspective of the wilderness road if we journeyed by truck. King arranged for us to ride with a load of his coal the nearly five hundred miles to Muncho Lake, just below the fabulous Yukon Territory. From there, he said, it would be an easy matter to arrange for transportation with another driver who enjoyed company.

We turned Cloud and Chinook out on range that October where the Barkleys promised to look after them if necessary. Dudley said he'd keep an eye on the cabin. We stored our saddles and a few other things with the Gethings. As the truck wheeled up the hill out of Hudson Hope, I felt the sudden desperate frightening need to cling to this land where we'd known such happiness. Brad looked grim, too. The vehicle with its heavy load thundered ahead.

When we slept at the Condill Hotel in Fort St. John that night, the furnace heat seemed stifling. The unaccustomed noise of strangers walking just beyond the thin wooden door made us jumpy.

"Maybe we are a little bushed at that," Brad muttered, rising to close the transom we'd opened in a useless effort to cool the room to our wilderness standards.

Yet, once we started north the next morning, excitement kept our spirits high. We liked the graveled and graded Alaska Highway, the sole overland route between civilization and this hemisphere's last great frontier. We'd been away from city people so long, however, that we were out of tune with the continually echoed desire we heard in dining rooms, filling stations, and trading posts to get there and back. Impatient tourists, tensely fighting for no sane reason every mile of a winding mountainous road not built for speed, first amused and then irked us.

"It doesn't make sense," Brad complained that night as we walked under the stars at Fort Nelson, where King Gething had freighted vital construction supplies by river during the embryonic days of the road north. "They drive up here ostensibly to see the country, and yet they can't spare time to look at it. A lot of them aren't even enjoying themselves. They don't want to be here. They just want to have been here."

"Remember what Thoreau said?" I asked. " 'The incessant anxiety and strain of some is a well-nigh incurable form of disease.' "

"That's right," he considered. "I guess we were a lot that way ourselves not so long ago. What gets me, though, is the lack of appreciation a lot of these pilgrims have."

"I wonder if it isn't more a lack of comprehension?" I mused. "After all, we've lived in the wilderness. We've spent a lot of days walking or riding maybe ten or twenty miles. We know what all this signifies. How long would it take to motor leisurely from Edmonton, say, to Teslin Lake halfway up the Highway?"

"Let's see, that's about 1300 miles," Brad replied. "Oh, a tourist could drive slowly enough to have plenty of fun and still make it less than a week."

"Exactly, and by city standards they wouldn't regard that as anything unusual," I agreed. "But do you recall what Bill Carter said when he told us about being in that detachment of Mounties who blazed a trail northward from Edmonton at the time of the Yukon gold rush?"

"Well, Bill said that prospectors who stampeded from Edmonton in 1898 over approximately this same route arrived at Teslin two years later." He stopped walking and just stood there in the night. A generator was humming somewhere to our right, and to the north the headlights of a truck lifted from behind a hill. "Most of these pilgrims haven't any such comparisons from which to draw, have they?"

Winter was already wailing southward from the Arctic. Snowbirds, only partially blanched in the thick muskeg country at the start of the journey, blended more and more completely with deepening drifts as we climbed into the majestically open Toad River country the second day out of Fort St. John.

"Indians didn't know what to make of it when bulldozers first started to smash through here," remarked our driver who'd handled one that spectacular winter of 1942-43 when this since continually improved life line to a million and a third square miles was being joined through mountains, muskegs, and mosquitoes in well under the year that many called impossible. "One of them ran terrified to tell his chief that God was coming through the bush, nostrils snorting and eyes shining, breaking down trees."

He had stories for every mile of the thoroughfare. Here a sourdough, new to the ways of service stations, had tried to add automobile oil through the tiny slit where the dip stick is inserted. There, he said—well, not exactly there but up at Lake Laberge—a party of stampeders broke through the ice,

and the Indian who claimed the water charged them fifty
cents apiece for bathing in it.

He arranged another ride for us when we stopped at Sum-
mit Lake for dinner the second day, and we changed trucks
near the great coiling Liard River late that afternoon. We
slept at Coal River the second night, at Swift River in the
fabulous Yukon Territory the third, and we geared down the
hill into Whitehorse on Saturday afternoon.

We liked this main gateway for the Klondike gold rush—
Whitehorse, now Mile 916, where the real Sam Magee's cabin
stands near a modern three story apartment house, built of
logs. Wind whirled around it now, catching up snow. "Please
close that door," one could almost hear the Robert W. Service character of that name protesting, as he had in the poem
when a friend opened the door of the boiler wherein he was
being cremated on the nearby shore of Lake Laberge. Since
Sam had left Plumtree, down in Tennessee, it was the first
time he'd been warm.

We liked the pulse-quickening hulks of old river boats
which had borne many a hopeful cheechako northward
along the Yukon River to Dawson City after George Car-
mack, a native of Massachusetts, had with his Indians found
gold on Bonanza Creek that historic August 17, 1896. A
single apparently worthless claim near that strike, sold by
swindlers for $600 to a drunken prospector who'd later wept
in vain for his money back, reputedly yielded the buyer almost two million dollars within four years. Newer wood
burning stern-wheelers were in dry docks, near the beached
Yukoner and Bonanza King, ready to paddle and winch their
way after break up in the spring on nine-day round trips to
the fringe of the Arctic Circle.

It annoyed us, though, to hear a table of New York-
ers grumbling when they were served milk mechanically
blended from powder and water instead of fresh milk—in
this country where men had once been glad to buy flour at

$50 a sack, eggs at $1 apiece, and vegetables at $15 a can when any were to be had.

"I've got to wheel on up to Burwash Landing tomorrow," our second driver greeted us when we met him on the road to Miles Canyon later that day. "I'll be back Monday, so you'll be able to catch the next train all right Tuesday. Better come along. It's worth the trip just to see Kluane Lake."

We did, and we agreed. The stark and savage grandeur of Kluane, Yukon mirror massively framed by Canada's loftiest crags, seemed third only after the upper Peace River and the Grand Canyon of the Colorado in our estimation among the continent's most beautiful magnificences. We turned there, not far from nearly four mile high Mt. Logan, almost eleven hundred miles up the Alaska Highway. We rode back past Destruction Bay and Haines Junction to Whitehorse.

We liked the 110-mile ride from this cosmopolitan crossroads by narrow gauge, trestle railroad past lovely and deserted Lake Bennett with its lone log church to Skagway, outlaw Soapy Smith's former Alaskan stronghold. Passengers now cross the mountains to the coast in plush comfort, although the exceedingly pretty wife of a greater San Francisco doctor did complain of the gaseous coal-burning stove in our coach—this within sight of the famed and frightful Chilkoot Trail over which some 25,000 stampeders had to struggle by foot in 1898. Many hadn't made it. One April snowslide, during that apical year on the world's gold-fever chart, had avalanched at least 65 to roaring destruction.

We liked the smooth, restful cruise down the sheltered Inside Passage to Vancouver, British Columbia. Juneau, Ketchikan, and other Alaskan ports otherwise inaccessible except by air were engrossing stops along this lake-like salt water route where bright glaciers, verdant forests, towering waterfalls, and cloud-scouring peaks drop sheer to a placid island-greened sea. But most of the tourists were complaining about the rainy weather.

Mining men, river boat captains, and other sourdoughs were predominant, however, on this next to the last boat of the season. We even met one of the former captains of the D. A. Thomas, HB.C. stern-wheeler that had once made scheduled runs up the Peace River as far as Hudson Hope. His chief engineer, also aboard, had been a clerk at Fort Graham upstream from Finlay Forks when King Gething had delivered mail there.

These old timers were not looking forward to a winter Outside if the conversations we heard from Tuesday to Saturday were any criterion. I, at least, listened with increasing doubt to their specific reasons for preferring the unspoiled works of God to man-made cities.

"Time to do what you want. Time never drags here, neither. After a couple of days Outside, I'm bored stiff. . . . Room to move around without getting shoved. . . . If you lay something down, some yahoo walks off with it. Up at my cabin, now, I never even lock the door. . . . Good food and an appetite that let's you enjoy it. . . . Even if you haven't got plenty of money, you can always live well in the bush. . . . Sleep good. . . . You can get a clean breath of air. . . . No rent. . . . What's that about being lord of all you survey? It's pretty true, anyway. In a city, on the other hand, you can't even step off the sidewalk to rest your feet in the grass. . . . All summer I hear pilgrims enthusing, 'Oh, heaven.' But every time I see their cities again, all I can think is, 'Oh, hell.' . . . The North is my home."

Brad and I talked about it that last morning in our deck cabin amidships, as we packed away comfortable bush garb and struggled into the clothes we'd originally worn north. Moths had found Brad's tweeds, which were too large at the waist now anyway and too small at the shoulders. His weight, however, was unchanged. As for me, a trip to the scales verified the fact that I'd gained twenty-six pounds in what Brad averred were not at all the wrong places and, five feet three and one-half inches tall, now weighed 127 pounds.

"Most of the luxuries and many of the so-called comforts are not only dispensable, but positive hindrances." Thoreau said it all a hundred years before. "Our life is frittered away with detail."

The cost of a thing is the amount of life which is required to be exchanged for it, immediately or in the long run. When one has obtained those essentials necessary to well being—food, shelter, warmth, and clothing—there is an alternative to struggling for the luxuries. That, Thoreau reasoned, is to adventure on life itself.

"It still makes sense," I admitted to Brad. "I wonder if we're not being foolish?"

"We'll have to find out for ourselves, I guess," was all he answered.

We disembarked in Vancouver, bought new clothes, crossed the border to Seattle where we secured an automobile, and drove southward in the van of the migrating swans.

CHAPTER THIRTY-ONE

RETURN TO NATURE

"I propose to brag as lustily as chanticleer in the morning if only to wake my neighbors up," Thoreau asserted, and so do we.

The clamor of birds winging northward, free as air, made us sit up soberly one city night and take stock. It came to this. We were working harder than we wanted, at things we didn't like to do. Why? In order to afford the sort of existence we didn't care to live!

"If a man does not keep pace with his companions, perhaps it is because he hears a different drummer." Distant throaty cries sounded hoarsely against a background of restless city movement. "Let him step to the music which he hears, however measured or far away."

The clangor of the departing birds made me suddenly afraid, perhaps because it blended so with impressions of a river now bright with ice cakes, of poplar buds bursting open on intense sweet mornings with the noise of popcorn, and of grass and wild foods flaming up like a spring fire—as if the earth were sending forth an inward heat to greet the returning sun.

I wanted again "to live deep and suck out all the marrow of life." I throbbed to be once more as free as air. Desperately, I ached to return to our home in the woods before something might happen to prevent us.

"We need the tonic of wilderness—to wade sometimes in marshes where the bittern and meadow hen lurk, and hear the booming of snipe; to smell the whispering sedge where only some wilder and more solitary fowl builds her nest, and the mink crawls with its belly close to the ground."

The words struck like a precisely inked rubber stamp against a still unwritten page of our life, and it was is if there drifted through the room the pleasant stench of wood smoke such as had never entirely escaped from some of our clothes. More than ever I realized the truth of what Thoreau had written, and I felt the almost frightened urge to hurry.

"We can never have enough of nature." It seemed as if time was moving inexorably past us along with the disappearing birds, although Thoreau's sentences seemed to enclose it momentarily like a frame. "We must be refreshed by the sight of inexhaustible vigor, vast and titantic features, the wilderness with its living and decaying trees, the thundercloud, the rain."

Like one who suddenly realizes he's been lost a long time, I wanted to run. When I tried to speak, my voice was uncertain. A lot of memories came crowding back, clear and poignant as bars of a remembered song. I found myself trying to shut them off, struggling to put my mind on something impersonal such as the present noise of traffic and the way a passing automobile spread rivulets of light across the plastered ceiling.

"Brad?" I begged when I could more nearly trust my words, and I waited for him to answer me. "Brad, don't you feel it, too?"

"Yes," he said finally. "But, then, I always have for myself." And then he waved an arm. "Here you don't have to scrub clothes, or get your hands sticky with pine pitch, or walk six miles for mail, or . . ."

I drew a quick breath. It was almost a sob, and I bit at my lips to steady them.

"Brad," I interrupted, and I had to whisper it because of the lump in my throat, "don't you want . . . ?" My voice broke, and I found myself reaching for him as if frightened. When he held me against him, I realized my cheek was wet with tears. "Don't you want to go home, too, Brad?"

The way he held me took my thoughts back to that decisive afternoon on Gloucester Street. I still couldn't speak. Then other words filled the choked silence; words strangely vehement, for the arms about me were so soothing.

"Sure, Vena," he said, almost harshly. "Sure, I feel it? But I practically forced you into going once. I didn't ever want to do that again, now not that you were able to decide for yourself. Besides. . . . Well, I still don't understand how Thoreau went wrong. He must have been wrong in leaving the woods when all that meant so much to him. Yet he was so right in everything else."

"But he was never really wrong, not in real life. That's where we made our mistake." I managed to smile, and I lifted my face. His questioning lips touched mine, warm and alive. "Thoreau left his cabin, yes. He didn't mention the rest of it in that book we have, but I've finally been reading more about him as we always said we would."

"What do you mean?" Brad asked.

"Thoreau moved only as far as Concord where he used to walk regularly from the cabin, anyway," I said. "He spent the rest of his life roaming about the same woods, the same fields, and the same Walden Pond."

Brad and I returned to Hudson Hope. It was as if we'd both been away a long time, and now we were back together once more. Perhaps we would need the brief tense contrast of cities again, I knew. Yet here, I realized, could be our only permanent home—where we could dwell like king and queen on an average ten dollars a week, where despite a small income we could build up such a savings account as was improbable elsewhere, and where, free as air, we could stretch and breathe and really live.

The first sounds of the late northern spring were all about us. Here the year was beginning with younger hope than ever. Faint silvery warblings lifted over woodlands and bare moist fields, from tanager and goldfinch, as if the last flakes of winter were tinkling as they fell.

Horses whinnied at us from a greening hillside. I walked up to Cloud as I always could, and then Brad managed with a succulent handful of vetch to entice the warier Chinook. We slipped our belts around their necks by which to lead them. At the Gethings we picked up our saddlery, and although everyone seemed as glad to see us as we were to be near them once more, they understandingly did not seek to delay us now. We rode toward home.

The swift sinking swish of snow paced us when the trail curved inland, for there chinooks and the sun had not yet vanquished the white remainders of winter. It was still a startling experience to witness an apparently solid crust ripple and settle ahead of our horses' crunching feet.

Blades of grass, which Thoreau called the symbol of perpetual youth, were bright green ribbons along the exposed areas beside the river, each lifting its spear of last year's hay with the fresh life below. Cloud's stride roughened, lengthened, and then eased into a lop. Chinook galloped a neck in front of him. Ahead, where the early evening shadows of trees spread like lace on its roof, gleamed our cabin.

The bliss and security of the moment were like a dam behind which flooding emotions suddenly overflowed into old, long unused sluiceways—for it was as if some things had been cut in stone upon my memory. I heard that train clackity-clack-clack-clacking out of the familiar echoes of the North Station into snow that stung frosting windows. I felt the release of carefree laughter when, after being cleared by Customs in Montreal, I'd first realized we were beyond turning back. I heard the musical clicking of horses' shoes that first Hudson Hope morning and once more saw my husband, whom I'd thought to be in bed beside me, starting alone up river.

There were the noises again of that first night in the Silent Places, the way the very tools had sung when we'd built our wilderness home, the bang the newly hung door made after its latch string had slipped from my fingers, the crackle of my first outdoor cooking fire, and the terrifying memory of thunderous falling shapes when we'd headed back through Box Canyon that second time into driving snow as thick as cotton batting.

The first morning I'd met Dudley Shaw was vivid in my mind. So was the night when Brad and I had fallen asleep with the thermometer outside registering more than ninety degrees below freezing, only to be awakened by the sound of water dripping from the roof. It was almost as if I were dancing again in Ted Boynton's old restaurant, and I felt surprised once more at the inside of the Cuthill's home and delighted at the unparalleled doors of a Hudson's Bay Company trading post.

I felt myself shrinking anew from the crushing walls that confronted me when I fell through the ice. I saw the cow moose swimming backwards down river with her calf, the huge bear edging past us to join her twin cubs, the grim skeletons beside that mountain lake, and the pair of yellow-eyed wolves that had appeared on the same fresh game trail we were following. There was the unforgettable sweetness of the evening Brad had come home with our first check, the rugged gentleness of the river cruise, the incredible greenish-blue of the glacial lake, the wild fruits and vegetables, trout and Arctic grayling, sizzling moose steaks, and the wonderful and awesome journey through Rocky Mountain Canyon and the nesting geese we'd heard afterwards. Recollections of that first Christmas Brad and I had spent in the wilderness made my eyes misty all over again.

"Here we are, darling," Brad was saying delightedly, as hoofs drew platinum splashes from the brook. He steadied Cloud's head while I dismounted. "Here we are, back home."

A coal oil lamp was once more our electricity, I knew, a pair of pails our water system. There were other inconveniences, too. Well, maybe some folks would call them that. We had before we'd realized they're also freedoms. If one doesn't have running water, there's no worry about meters and bursting pipes. If stoves crackle with your own wood, high fuel costs and labor-management difficulties are something to plague the other fellow.

"Here," I heard Brad say almost shyly. I saw he was extending a long oblong fold of paper toward me with one hand, as he slipped Cloud's halter rope from my saddle horn with the other. "Here's what I've been trying to get for you ever since that first Christmas here, Vena. It came awhile back, but I figured this would be the right time to give it to you."

"The Fractional South East quarter of the Fractional South East quarter of Lot one hundred and forty-nine, Peace River District," I read, eyes darting from the brilliant red seal in the lower right corner to the black Old English lettering at the top. "Certificate of Indefeasible Title."

"It's really ours now just as you always wanted, this land along the river on both sides of Bull Creek." He motioned with a hand. "I finally managed to buy it from the Provincial Government. It cost five dollars an acre."

The faint distant cries of migrating birds caught my attention, even as our cabin door creaked open. Wild wings flapped exultantly nearer, the sound mingling vaguely with the music of wilderness water and the muttering of trees. Then we saw at the same moment a great uneven angle chalked against an aquamarine sky tremulous with the Northern Lights.

"Swans!" Brad said. "Wild swans!"

"Well, they needn't call for us again on the way back." I waved at them, then drew utterly happy within the warmth of my husband's arms as he bore me into our home in the woods. "We've settled."

END